Voices against Slavery

(((VOICES)))

Voices against Slavery

Catherine House

Anthony Benezet

Olaudah Equiano

Granville Sharp

William Wilberforce

Elizabeth Heyrick

Sam Sharpe

Harriet Tubman

Harriet Beecher Stowe

David Livingstone

Baroness Cox

CHRISTIAN FOCUS

This edition © copyright 2006 Catherine House
Christian Focus Publications
ISBN: 1-84550-145-4

Published by Christian Focus Publications Ltd,
Geanies House, Fearn, Tain, Ross-shire,
IV20 1TW, Scotland, Great Britain.
www.christianfocus.com
email:info@christianfocus.com

Cover design by Danie van Straaten
Printed and bound by Nørhaven AS

For Mum and Dad

"I believe that all persons,
but more especially the youth,
ought to know by what wicked
and corrupt views and methods
the slave trade is carried on,
and the curse that will attend
those who, for selfish ends,
engage in it in any

degree whatever."

Anthony Benezet
December 1757

CONTENTS

TIMELINE
1772-2007

Voices against slavery is a book that tells some of the stories of Christian people who have fought against slavery at different times and in different ways. The following timeline shows when some of the events described in these stories actually happened.

1772	The legal case brought by James Somerset, leads to the ending of slavery within England. Slavery remains legal in British colonies. Anthony Benezet writes, *Some Historical Account of Guinea*
1781	132 enslaved people are murdered by the Captain of the ship *Zong*. The court case that followed makes people aware of the true nature of the slave trade.
1787	Granville Sharp helps to form the Society for the Abolition of the Slave Trade.
1789	Olaudah Equiano publishes his book, *The Interesting Narrative of the Life of Olaudah Equiano*, or *Gustavus Vassa, the African*.
	William Wilberforce gives his first major abolition speech before the British parliament.
1807	Slave trade abolished in Britain.
1808	Slave trade abolished in the United States.
1823	Slave uprising in Demerara.
1824	Elizabeth Heyrick publishes her pamphlet, *Immediate not Gradual Abolition*.
1832	Slave uprising in Jamaica, led by Samuel Sharpe.
	William Knibb, a missionary in Jamaica, campaigns for the abolition of slavery in Britain.

1833   British parliament passes the Abolition of Slavery Act.

1834   Slavery is abolished throughout the British colonies.

1849   In America, Harriet Tubman runs away from slavery.

1850   Declaration of the Fugitive Slave Law in United States.
        Harriet Tubman starts her work helping people escape
        from slavery.

1852   Uncle Tom's Cabin by Harriet Beecher Stowe is published.

1861-1865 The American Civil War leads to the abolition of slavery in
        the United States.

1873   David Livingstone dies in Africa.
        The Sultan of Zanzibar closes the slave market on the
        island and makes the slave trade by sea illegal
        in his territories.

1948   The United Nations adopts the Universal Declaration of
        Human Rights. Article 4 prohibits all forms of slavery and
        the slave trade.

1999   Baroness Cox reports on the existence of slavery within
        Sudan.

2007   200th Anniversary of the transatlantic slave trade and its
        abolition.
        The fight against modern day slavery continues.

❧ Anthony Benezet ❧

THE CLOCK ABOVE THE MARKET SQUARE WAS ABOUT to strike midnight. Thick clouds hid the moon, and a cold wind threatened to bring the first winter snow. In the empty street, someone was quietly knocking on John Benezet's door. Taking a candle, the merchant went to lift the latch. "Who's there?" he whispered.

"Pierre," came the reply. A young man, wrapped in a dark wool cloak, stepped into the hallway.

"Did anyone follow you?" John asked as he bolted the door firmly.

"No, the soldiers were drinking. But I don't have much time. I've heard that you have been denounced as a traitor to the King. Any day now, the soldiers will come to take your house and property."

John Benezet sat with his head in his hands. "But what have I done?" he sighed. "All I want to do is to worship the Lord and to follow God's teaching in the Bible. Why can't we be left alone to worship as we want?"

"You must make a plan!" the young man paced the floor. "Remember there are other countries where you can worship freely."

"Yes, I know that's true. But it's illegal to try and cross the French borders. I have a young family to think about. My wife is pregnant and

11

shouldn't be travelling at such a time. Let me pray about this news. God will guide us. He will show us what to do."

"My friends and I are here to help," Pierre said as he prepared to leave. "The French government can take our houses, destroy our Bibles and exile our pastors. But they can never take away our faith. You know how to reach me. But don't delay, because you will be watched. If you leave it too late you will be unable to flee."

As the young man vanished into the shadows, John kneeled on the cold stone floor to pray, "Lord you know my heart. Do not forsake me now. But give me the strength to stay faithful to you until the end…"

Judith Benezet stirred restlessly as the weak winter sun broke through the clouds over the French town of St. Quentin. With her eyes closed, she reached out to her husband but the bed was empty. Suddenly she was wide-awake. "John?" she called. There was no answer.

For a moment, Judith feared the worst. Perhaps the soldiers had come in the night. Had they taken her husband? She flung back the blankets and reached for her gown.

At that moment the door creaked open. John stood in the doorway looking exhausted, his eyes red from lack of sleep. Without a word, he hugged his wife and then quietly began to explain. "My dear, the time has come for us to leave the country. I have been praying and believe that we must act immediately."

Judith wanted to cry, but the tears would not come. She had already cried for her friends who had fled their homes to escape religious persecution. She had already cried at the news of the murder of some of those who had been caught. She had already cried for the young men who had refused to turn from their Christian faith and who were now in prison. Yet for herself, there were no tears. Instead a feeling of peace filled her heart.

Despite being heavily pregnant, Judith felt calm about her husband's announcement. She had been preparing for this day. Locked away in a secret cupboard was a small bundle. Inside the bundle was a bag of gold, a warm blanket and a Bible.

"Our dear Lord will guide us to a new home. I am ready to leave," Judith reassured her husband.

It was a cold night in February, when Pierre entered the Benezet's house again. This time he did not come through the front door. Instead he had slipped over the back wall of their house and now stood waiting in the kitchen. A little boy of two years old looked up at him.

"Hello Anthony, look what I have for you." Pierre opened his hand slowly as the child watched. In Pierre's hand were three of Anthony's favourite sweets.

"Here is one sweet for you now. Soon we are going on a walk across the fields. If you promise me not to make a noise until we reach the woods, I will give you the other two sweets."

At that point a girl dressed in a thick woollen dress ran into the room.

"And of course Marie, I have some sweets for you as well," Pierre said to Anthony's sister. "Now remember, both of you must not make a sound."

Anthony was too young to understand why his family was leaving their house that night. Yet as his father carried him across the frozen fields, he sensed that something was very wrong. However, only when they reached the cover of the wood, did he begin to cry.

"Shh! Don't cry!" his mother whispered to him as she climbed up into a waiting wagon.

"Perhaps this will help!" Pierre said as he passed more sweets to each of the children. As the horses pulled away, Anthony stopped crying and within a short time had fallen fast asleep on his mother's lap.

The Benezet family travelled as quickly as they could across the French countryside towards the border. Keeping to quiet roads well away from towns and villages, they managed to avoid the roadblocks and the soldiers.

Pierre had made this journey before. He knew that the most dangerous part still lay ahead. As the border crossing came into sight, he turned to John Benezet.

"From here you must walk. Let me go first. I will speak to the guard."

John took his wife's hand and bent to kiss his two children. He knew that if they were stopped at the border, he might never see his family again. The children would be taken from them. Judith would be imprisoned in a convent. He could be executed or forced to work as a slave on board the French King's ships. "Oh God, be with us in this our hour of need…" he prayed. "We are ready, Pierre. Let's go."

Pierre reached under the seat of the wagon and pulled out a bundle of rags. His face looked white and tense. Unwrapping the cloth, he took out a pistol and a leather pouch. Pierre quickly slipped the pistol into his belt and walked immediately away from the Benezet family. He did not want to discuss his actions with John. Instead he pushed his hair back from his face, took a deep breath and walked confidently towards the waiting guard.

"Who goes there?" shouted the soldier.

At that point, Pierre tossed his cloak back over his shoulders. The soldier saw immediately that the young man was carrying a pistol in one hand. It was ready to be fired. In the other hand was a pouch containing gold coins.

With the pistol pointing at the soldier, Pierre challenged him. "Choose!"

For a moment the guard stood shocked, unsure how to reply. Pierre continued.

"These are good people who are being persecuted simply because of their religion. You can choose to let them pass safely across the border. If you choose to do this, you will be rewarded with this bag of gold. Or you can choose to fight. If you do this, you will die!"

There was silence for a moment. The guard glanced at his own rifle. It lay useless against the wooden guard hut. He would never be able to reach it in time.

"Quick!" the guard replied. "My companion will be back any moment. Give me the gold and I will let them pass."

Pierre began to smile. "Not so quickly my friend. Let this family pass first, and then I will give you the gold!"

John Benezet, his wife and two children slipped quietly across the border that day into the Netherlands. A few weeks later Judith gave birth to her baby but the child did not survive. Shortly afterwards the Benezet family took a boat and crossed the sea to England as refugees. They made their home in London, where they were free to worship with other French Christians and where John Benezet could start his business once again. However, the Benezet family did not remain in London, there was still one more journey for them to make.

Anthony Benezet stood at the back of a smoke filled room, listening to a tall stranger. Anthony was now seventeen and training to be a merchant, like his father and uncle. The three of them had been invited to this meeting, to hear about life in the British colonies in North America.

"America is the land of opportunity. Don't miss out! Come and join our colony!" the stranger concluded his speech.

A poorly dressed man stood up. "It may be the land of opportunity, but how do we get there? The passage to America is so expensive."

"You don't need to worry about that," came the reply. "Sign a contract with us that you will work as a servant for four to ten years. When you arrive in America your master will pay your passage."

A murmur went around the room. Anthony's father and uncle stood to leave and Anthony followed. That evening the Benezet family discussed what they had heard.

"Let's go together!" Anthony's uncle declared. "So many of our friends have now sailed for America. We have enough money to pay for our passage, and we could expand our business there."

"God has always guided us as a family. If it is his will, then we will go," John Benezet replied.

Finally the decision was made and in 1731 the Benezet family set sail for America. Anthony Benezet stood on the deck and watched the English coast disappear out of sight. Below deck, his mother was trying to organise their trunks and arrange space for her seven children to sleep. The ship seemed very crowded and Judith prayed quietly that the winds would be strong and that the journey would be short. She had brought as much food as she could. Yet she knew that there was not enough to keep hunger away, and that after four weeks they would have to depend on the ship's supply.

Within a few days, Anthony also realised that their passage to America was going to be a difficult and unpleasant one. Down below deck, there was hardly any room to move. The pounding of the waves made him feel terribly sick. The drinking water was dirty and people began to fall ill with diarrhoea.

One morning Anthony woke up to the sobbing of a young woman. In her arms was a baby. "My child is dead, my child is dead," she cried helplessly. Her husband tried to comfort her, but she would not listen. "It's your fault, you should never have brought us on this ship."

Within a few days an elderly man also died. A short service was held before his body was dropped into the sea. Anthony stood and listened to the Bible reading. Silently he prayed to God, "If I survive this journey, show me what to do with my life. Help me to follow your paths and to trust you, whatever may happen."

Finally after five weeks at sea, land was sighted. Some passengers let out a cheer. Others knelt on the deck, thanking God for their arrival. Everyone wanted to celebrate the end of the sea journey.

"Look Daniel, there's Philadelphia," Anthony called his brother to the side of the ship as they sailed along the Delaware River. In the distance they could see the docks with their taverns, shops and warehouses.

"Do you think it will be like London?" Daniel asked his older brother.

"No," Anthony replied. "We're about to start a new life now. This will be a new world for us. It's going to be very different indeed."

Some things, however, did not change for Anthony. His family immediately set up business as merchants. They opened a shop, hired a warehouse and began to trade in luxury goods from London. Anthony was expected to play his role in the family business.

"Tidy the shelves, count the money, write up the ledgers!" came the orders. Anthony did as he was told; yet something inside didn't feel right. The years began to pass and that feeling of uneasiness grew.

"What's the matter, Anthony?" Daniel asked one day as he saw his brother sigh as he opened up the shop.

"I'm not sure, Daniel. But ever since I arrived in this country, I have felt that I should be doing something else with my life."

His brother laughed. "What else is there to do? We are all merchants! Father, Uncle James, your brothers ... and look at how successful we have become. What more could you want?"

"Well, actually… I think I would like to be a teacher," Anthony replied quietly.

Daniel shook his head. "You're so strange sometimes! You spend far too much time reading. It's not good for you. Here give me a hand. I need to move these furs into the warehouse."

Eventually at the age of twenty-five, Benezet made up his mind. He did what he really wanted to do and became a teacher.

At that time, school was often a boring and harsh place for children. There were no books and children learnt by simply repeating what the teacher said. Children were not allowed to play during school time and had to sit perfectly quiet whilst the teacher spoke. Many of these teachers were hardly educated themselves.

Children who did not behave well were punished. Boys had to remove their jackets and were then whipped with a rod. Girls were also punished by being hit across their legs or by being hit with a ruler. It was not surprising that children were often afraid of their teachers.

"I want my school to be different," Benezet tried to explain to the trustees of his school. "For one thing we need a better school room. The window is broken. It is too dark to work. And there is no room to play." The trustees agreed to mend the window and finally they built a new schoolroom.

However, that was not the only change that Benezet wanted to see in his school. He took the rods that were used to punish children and broke them in two. At home, he explained to his wife Joyce, "I don't need rods in my school. They are cruel and unnecessary. I believe that teachers should be kind and gentle. If you treat children well, then they will learn how to be good and kind themselves."

It was not surprising, therefore, that Benezet's school was extremely popular. However, some of the children still liked to test their schoolmaster. Surely, Benezet could not be kind all the time!

The classroom was strangely silent, as the short plainly dressed teacher came through the door. Two boys began to giggle at the back. Benezet glanced quickly at his pupils and then stared down at his table. There in a trap was a mouse. It was tied and unable to move. The little creature was squealing with fear. Next to the mouse was a note with the words:

> "I stand here, my honest friends
> For stealing cheese and candle-ends."

"Poor thing! Who put you here?" the teacher asked the mouse and then looked sternly at each pupil in turn. However, Benezet had no trouble in identifying the guilty boys.

"Stand on the desk!" he commanded them as he carefully released the mouse and let it go.

The two boys at the back of the class waited to hear what their punishment would be. Perhaps this would finally force the gentle teacher to bring back his rods to the classroom.

For the rest of the lesson, Benezet changed his lesson plan. "This morning, we will study the importance of kindness," he announced.

At the end of the class, the two boys were kept behind. "You must be punished for your actions," Benezet spoke firmly. "For the rest of the week you will have to stay behind after school and do extra work."

At the end of each day Benezet returned home to his wife, ate a quick supper and began work again.

"James, you're early," Benezet welcomed a child into his lounge. James Forten was the son of an African American woman who had been freed from slavery. Benezet remembered the first time he had met her.

"Mr. Benezet, I want my son to go to school. But there is no school for black children. Can you help me?"

The teacher had listened to her plea and as a result had started an evening school for children from African American families. Soon he had a group of eager pupils, who were learning to read and write for the very first time.

At the end of the evening, when all his pupils had left, he turned as usual to his lesson preparation for the next day.

"Anthony, you work too hard," Joyce would often say. Her husband would then take her hand and reply with the same words.

"Jesus commanded us to love one another as he loved us. We can never do too much to show that love."

Benezet was working in his vegetable garden when he heard his wife calling to him.

"Quick, come! The Acadian ships have been sighted. They will be in the harbour soon."

The Acadians were a group of people who had originally come from France but who had made their home in Nova Scotia, which today is part of Canada. The English commanders feared that these people would not be loyal to the English authorities. So they forced the Acadian people onto ships and took them away from their homes in Nova Scotia to towns in America and England. Four hundred and sixty four people were sent by ship to Philadelphia.

Picking up his hat, Benezet went to call upon other members of the Society of Friends who were also known as Quakers. These Christians believed that if they listened quietly to God, then he would speak to their hearts and show them what to do. Helping the poor and needy was an important part of their faith.

"We must be at the dock to welcome these poor refugees," Benezet explained to his fellow Quakers. He knew the stories of his own family's escape from France and how they had been refugees. Many of his friends were also refugees from Germany. He knew the suffering and the needs of people forced from their homes.

Silently Benezet and his friends watched the four ships with their large white sails make their way into the harbour. One ship was the Royal Navy escort. The other three contained the imprisoned people and the few belongings that they had been allowed to carry with them.

Before Benezet could board the ships, they had to be inspected by the harbour master. However, his inspection did not last long.

"I'm afraid you can't go aboard," the harbour master informed the waiting men. "There's smallpox amongst those people. The Arcadians will have to stay on board for another month until the illness has passed."

"But we must get on board and see what help these people need. It is our Christian duty to offer what assistance we can."

Eventually after more arguments, the harbour master agreed to their request. On board one of the ships, Benezet climbed down the ladder into the lower deck. The smell was overpowering. Women, children and men sat exhausted from their sea voyage and from their despair. Benezet greeted the travellers in French.

"You speak French?" one of the men approached Benezet with relief.

"Yes, I do my friend. My family used to live in France."

"Please help us..." a woman reached out her arms towards him.

"What do you need?" Benezet asked gently.

"Clothes. It is so cold and we do not have enough shirts or socks."

"Blankets and sheets!" someone else called out.

Suddenly everyone wanted to talk to Benezet and to share his or her problems.

"We were tricked by the English," an old man tried to explain with tears in his eyes. "We had done nothing against the English, yet their soldiers took everything. They waited until we had finished the harvest and then they arrested all the men. Now we have been taken from our homes, and our houses and farms destroyed. We will surely die..."

Benezet and his friends did what they could to help. One day, Joyce met her husband after school with a worried look. "There have been thieves in our house," she exclaimed. "Two blankets have disappeared."

The teacher smiled. "Don't worry my dear. We haven't had thieves. I gave the blankets away to some Acadians. They are in such need, I couldn't turn them away."

Benezet and the Society of Friends helped the Arcadians to build some simple houses. However, the winter was harsh and disease spread easily. Large numbers of the people who had come from Canada continued to die. The families turned to Benezet once again.

"Give us coffins so that we can bury our dead with dignity," they asked.

Also arriving at the ports of America against their wills, were increasing numbers of enslaved Africans. They had been stolen from their homes and were then sold into a life of hard and never ending work. Owned by a master, these people lost their freedom and were treated as things rather than as human beings.

Benezet knew about slavery because he had read the leaflets written by other Quakers condemning the slave trade. The ending of the slave trade was something he totally agreed with. Yet now, as he taught black children and made friends with their families his knowledge changed into a deeper understanding.

He decided to find out everything he could about slavery and the slave trade. This was made easier because Philadelphia was a seaport and many ships from the West Indies came to the town's docks. He met and talked with black sailors, enslaved people, merchants and travellers. He also read everything he could about Africa. What Benezet found out about the slave trade shocked him deeply.

The tired teacher sat looking at the piece of paper lying on his desk. How can I possibly write about these awful things, Benezet thought to himself? Yet he knew that he must. People didn't know the truth about what was happening in the plantations in the West Indies. Someone had to tell them. He began to describe how slaves were treated on the Island of Jamaica. Carefully he wrote down what he had learnt.

"When slaves rebel, they are punished by being burnt to death. If they do not work hard enough they are whipped with pieces of wood.

They are given a small piece of land on which to grow their own food. Yet Africans are only allowed half a day at the end of the week, to work in these gardens. And this day is Sunday when people should be allowed to rest and worship God.

Africans in the West Indies work from daybreak until noon. Then they work from two o'clock until dark. Even then they are not allowed to go home. They may have to collect fodder for their master's horses or collect fuel. Their owners work them as hard as possible and yet hardly give them enough food and clothes to live. In Jamaica, six out of ten Africans brought to the island do not survive the first three years.

And who are these people whom the planters are treating with such cruelty? They are his brothers! His neighbours! They are the children of our heavenly Father, for whom Christ died. One day each slave owner will have to give an account to God. How will they explain what they have done?"

Benezet carried the finished manuscript to his friend, Christopher Sower, the publisher. "Will people read what I have written?" he wondered to himself. "Will it change anything?"

He need not have worried. Throughout America and Europe, people began to read Anthony Benezet's leaflets. At that time, most people did not question the use of slaves. Slavery was part of life. However, after reading Benezet's writing many people began to think differently.

The Quakers themselves were amongst the first to act. By 1758, the Society of Friends in Philadelphia had condemned slavery and expelled anyone who owned slaves. By 1780, the State government of Pennsylvania had passed the Gradual Abolition of Slavery Act. In Britain, Benezet's books were published and people were beginning to listen to what he had to say about the injustice of slavery. Slowly more and more people began to speak out against slavery because of what they read.

The news spread quickly through the town. "Anthony Benezet is dying," the message passed from person to person. A crowd of people began to assemble outside his house, waiting for the latest information.

At the age of 71, Anthony Benezet knew that it was time for him to die. Turning to his wife Joyce, he took her hand. "We have lived a long time together in love and in peace," he sighed. The next day, he was dead.

His body was taken to the Quaker cemetery for burial. Along the side of the road, gathered the people of Philadelphia. Amongst them were over 400 black people.

"Father, why are we here?" asked one little boy. "What's happening?"

"Anthony Benezet has died. He was the man who taught me to read," came the reply. "But more than that, he has raised his voice against the the slave trade. So today we have come to pay our respects, and to pray for the freedom of all our people."

At a Glance: Anthony Benezet

In the 1750s, Anthony Benezet began to speak out about the slave trade. As a result, the Society of Friends (Quakers) became the first Christian group to totally reject the ownership of enslaved people. Anthony also encouraged people outside America, to campaign against the slave trade. In England, Granville Sharp and Thomas Clarkson read Benezet's anti-slavery pamphlets and helped to start the abolition movement in Britain.

Benezet believed in equality and encouraged the education of African Americans. He set up a school for black children in Philadelphia and taught there himself. In 1775 Benezet founded the Society for the Relief of Free Negroes Unlawfully Held in Bondage. Later this became the Pennsylvania Society for Promoting the Abolition of Slavery.

Benezet died in 1784, aged 71. At his funeral 400 black people came to mourn and to honour him for his fight for the rights and freedom of Africans.

Fact File: Slavery in Africa

1 Slavery existed in Africa hundreds of years before the start of the African-European slave trade.

2 Many slaves sold within Africa were prisoners of war or criminals. However, slaves within Africa were often treated as part of a household and could improve their status through hard work.

3 Slaves were also taken across Africa by Arab traders and sold in North Africa, Asia and the Middle East.

4 When Europeans arrived in Africa in the 1400s the demand for slaves began to grow. At first these slaves were taken to Europe. Then they began to be taken in large numbers across the Atlantic to countries in South America, North America and the Caribbean.

Faith in action

Anthony Benezet's faith was centred on the teachings of Jesus Christ, particularly the words of Jesus Christ from the book of Matthew: 'So in everything, do to others what you would have them do to you, for this sums up the Law and the Prophets.' (Matthew 7:12)

Benezet asked people to think about how they would feel if someone made them a slave. If they did not want to live in slavery, then why were they enslaving others? The challenge of Jesus' teaching remains the same. Do we treat people, as we would like to be treated? Do we care about others, as we care about ourselves?

Talk about it

Why is it important to know about the history of the slave trade? Learning about the past helps us to build a better future. Learning about our history, also helps us to understand why the world is like it is today. However, many people still do not know much about the slave trade or the impact it has had on our world. Have you been taught about the slave trade at school? What did you learn? Do you think that all children should be taught about this subject? Why?

Make your voice heard

Everyone has a right to freedom and their human rights. It is unjust to make some people work for no or little pay, so that others can live a good life. It is unjust to separate families and force people to leave their homes. Other human rights issues include: the fight against poverty; the fight for fair trade; how to look after the environment and our natural resources. Everyone has a part to play in working for a just and fair world. No one's efforts are insignificant. Ask yourself 'How will I make my voice heard?'

One thing you can do is pray for freedom and justice. Harriet Beecher Stowe (Chapter 8) asked her readers to pray for God's Holy Spirit to give power for the fight against slavery. She also asked people to pray for enslaved people and to support those people who had gained their freedom.

Olaudah Equiano

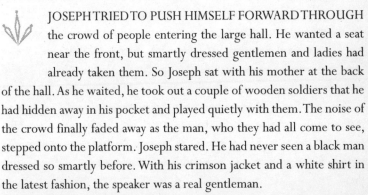 JOSEPH TRIED TO PUSH HIMSELF FORWARD THROUGH the crowd of people entering the large hall. He wanted a seat near the front, but smartly dressed gentlemen and ladies had already taken them. So Joseph sat with his mother at the back of the hall. As he waited, he took out a couple of wooden soldiers that he had hidden away in his pocket and played quietly with them. The noise of the crowd finally faded away as the man, who they had all come to see, stepped onto the platform. Joseph stared. He had never seen a black man dressed so smartly before. With his crimson jacket and a white shirt in the latest fashion, the speaker was a real gentleman.

"My name is Olaudah Equiano," the speaker announced with pride.

"And tonight I want to tell you the story of my life. As I look back, I have had many adventures, many trials and many disappointments. Yet from an early age, I learnt to see the hand of God at work in even the smallest of events. And from that belief, I have tried to learn from the things that have happened to me so that I might be a wiser and better person. My prayer is that through what has happened to me, I will act justly, love mercy and walk humbly with God." The crowd were now quietly listening as Equiano began to tell his story.

"My life began in West Africa. I was part of a large and happy family. Yet even as a child, I had one fear: the fear of being kidnapped and taken into slavery. When our parents went to work in the fields, all the children used to play together for safety. One of us would keep watch in case a kidnapper came. One day it was my turn to climb a tree and to keep watch. I saw someone making his way silently to us. Raising the alarm, I climbed down the tree as fast as I could. The older boys knew immediately what to do. They surrounded the intruder, managed to overpower him and then tied him up to await the anger of our returning parents.

"However, the next time a kidnapper slipped into our village, I would not be so fortunate. Three African slave traders came silently one day, as my sister and I were playing alone. Before I could reach for my spear or even cry out in alarm, they had grabbed us, tied us up and were forcing us along the path away from our home and family. My life as a happy child had abruptly come to an end and my life as a slave had begun.

"At first I was sold to a chief who treated me well. My job was to stoke the fire, so that he could do his work as a blacksmith. Yet whilst I worked, my thoughts were with my family. I missed my mother and friends desperately and so planned how I could escape and return to them.

"Then one morning I took my chance and ran off into the forest. I could hear my master looking for me, but I hid in the undergrowth and no one found me. Yet as night fell, I began to panic.

"In the distance, the call of wild animals seemed to be coming closer and closer. It was so dark that I could no longer see what I was stepping on. Every moment I feared that I might stumble upon a snake. The forest seemed so dense that my plans to find my way home now seemed foolish. With nothing to eat or drink, there was only one path I could tread. Exhausted and hungry, I returned to my master's compound and immediately fell asleep in front of the open fire. Once more my master showed me kindness and did not punish me for running away. However, tragedy was about to strike the family, which would have serious consequences for me. Soon after my return, the daughter of the house fell ill and died. My master was broken hearted. He decided to sell me.

"Once again I found myself travelling through unknown countryside, further and further away from my home. Once again I was sold into a kind family who treated me as one of their own children. Yet once again I was sold on. On this occasion my fate would not be so kind. I was taken to the coast where I saw crashing waves for the very first time. And for the first time, I saw a ship anchored off shore, waiting for its cargo to be loaded. In my ignorance I did not know what this ship was, or what cargo it was destined to carry."

As Equiano described the ship, Joseph suddenly remembered something that had happened a few weeks earlier. He had been walking down the street with his sister Clara, when he saw a crowd outside a shop front. Curious to see what everyone was looking at, he managed to find a way to the front. There in the shop window was a large poster. The poster was a drawing of the inside of the slave ship *Brookes*.

Joseph had stared at the ship and the tiny drawings of African people. Rows of slaves were shown packed in like animals with hardly room to lie down. Each slave was shackled to another by iron cuffs around the ankles and wrists.

For a moment Joseph paused silently. He knew that slaves were taken across the Atlantic ocean in ships, but he had never thought about how it was done, or about how awful it was for the thousands of men, women and children who experienced this journey. Now looking at the picture, Joseph was shocked. Yet what he was about to hear from Equiano would shock him even further.

"The African slave traders took me on board the ship where I was prodded and poked by men whose very appearance filled me with terror. Their skin was light, their hair was long and they spoke in a language that I could not understand. Looking around the ship I saw other black people, standing chained, their faces filled with sorrow and despair.

"In one corner of the ship there was a large copper pot on a fire. My mind was filled with the thought that these ugly men were going to eat us. Terrified at this possibility, I fainted and fell onto the ship's deck. The men, who were selling me, woke me up and tried to reassure me that I was not to be eaten. However, I could see now that all hope of escape was gone. Yet my despair was to deepen further when I was taken below the deck where other slaves were being kept.

"Below deck, in the heat and the dirt, the smell was unbearable. In such conditions, I no longer wanted to live and refused all food. However, I was soon to learn that a slave is not even free to stop eating or to choose death. Two white men tried to get me to eat. When I refused, they took me up on deck, tied me up and flogged me.

"As I had never seen the sea before, I was afraid of the water around the ship. Yet at that moment I longed to run and throw myself over the side of the boat. However, the sailors were used to slaves trying to jump off the ship and so they watched us carefully. Around the edge of the boat were nets to stop people jumping overboard. Those who attempted it were severely punished.

"Eventually I found some slaves who were from my own people. A couple of the women looked after me and they explained what was happening. "We are being taken to the white man's country to work for them," they explained. I was not afraid of work, but I was afraid of the white men who acted with such cruelty even to their own people.

"Once when we were allowed on deck for some fresh air, we saw one of the white sailors being beaten. He was flogged with a large rope and his injuries were so great that he died. Without a thought, his companions took the body and threw it overboard.

Finally the day came when the white men had finished buying their human cargo. Hundreds of slaves were shut below deck, whilst the anchor was raised and the ship headed out into deep sea. Below deck it had been bad before but now it was suffocating. There were so many people that we could hardly move. The smell and the heat meant that it was difficult to breathe. The men had been put into chains, which rubbed their legs and arms, causing pain and great discomfort. Some of the slaves began to die; their groans were added to the cries of women and children.

I, too, began to fall ill and so was allowed back on deck. Because I was young, the white men did not put chains on me. Every day I watched dead bodies being brought up from the slave quarters and I wished that I too could die and escape the misery that I found myself in.

One day, two men who had been brought on to the deck hand-cuffed together, could take no more. Before the white men knew what was going on, they rushed together and somehow got over the nets. Another slave, who was lying ill, saw what had happened, and he too ran and jumped over ship. Once the sailors knew what was going on, we were all pushed back down into the hold. They launched a boat to try and recover the slaves. Two of them had drowned, but the other man was recaptured. He was beaten mercilessly for having tried to kill himself.

Eventually, after many weeks at sea, there was a loud shout from the white men. Land was in sight. We had arrived at the island of Barbados. Although the sailors were rejoicing, we were deeply afraid of what was to happen to us.

On landing, we were taken to a merchant's yard. Within a few days we were to be sold. On the bang of a drum, the buyers rushed into the yard, grabbing those slaves which they wanted to buy. The sale was chaotic and confusing. Mothers and children were separated. Families were spilt up and sold to different owners.

"On the ship that had brought me to the West Indies, were a group of brothers. When they saw that they were to be taken by different owners they cried out in anger:

"'You call yourself Christians, yet you ignore the teaching of your God who says that you should 'do to others what you would have them do to you.' Isn't it enough that you have stolen us from our country and our home, just so that we can work to make you rich? Yet now you take away our only source of comfort by separating us.'

Equiano paused for a moment as he remembered the distress of slaves being parted from their families. Then he turned again to his audience, "Why should parents be parted from their children, brothers from their sisters or husbands from their wives? Slavery is wretched enough and yet the separation of families increases the cruelty and the despair."

Equiano continued to question his audience. "What is it like to be a slave?" he asked. "Let me tell you what being a slave meant for one of my friends who lived in the West Indies.

"My friend worked hard for his master. Then during the short time that he was free from work, he loved to fish. One day I saw him on the harbour wall. He had a small pile of fish at his feet. Walking along the harbour were two white men. Laughing, they stopped by the slave, looked down at his fish and then walked off with them. My friend could do nothing to stop them taking his precious catch. Later that day he explained to me that this often happened to him.

"'Sometimes when a white man takes my fish, I go to my master. He is sometimes able to get them back for me. But many times my master takes the fish for himself. What can I do then? Who can I turn to for help? Who will give me my rights?' My friend paused for a moment and turned his eyes upward to the skies. 'I must look above to God Almighty for my rights,' he concluded.

"I felt the sadness in his heart and from all I had seen and experienced myself could only agree with him. 'We must look to God for there is no justice on this earth for a slave.'

"That is what it is like to be a slave," Equiano sighed. "It is to be without freedom and it is to be without justice."

No one moved or said a word. The well-dressed lady who was sitting next to Joseph touched the broch pinned to her dress. On the broch was a picture of a slave in chains, kneeling on the ground begging for freedom. Joseph knew that this was the symbol of the many people who were supporting an end to the slave trade; a trade that he was now beginning to understand for himself. Joseph continued to listen carefully as Equiano explained how he had managed to buy his own freedom.

"Today I stand in front of you as a free man. Yes, slaves do gain their freedom but the numbers are so small compared to the thousands and thousands who live and die in slavery. And those slaves who do gain their freedom find that the walk to freedom is a rough road.

"As a boy I was bought by Captain Pascal and sailed for England. He was a kind master and treated me well. On his ship I fought against the French, running up and down the gundeck with powder for the cannons. At any moment I knew I could be killed. During that time I earned a small wage from the British Navy and also received part of the prize money when we captured an enemy ship. Yet I was not to receive that money, instead my master would claim it on my behalf. I, therefore, wrongly assumed that when the war came to an end my master would grant me my freedom. However, as we sailed towards London, it soon became clear that he had other plans for me. Against my wishes I was taken and put on a boat bound for the West Indies. My friends tried to help me, but their attempts to rescue me failed. I cried out to God for help, 'Do not forget me, O Lord. I will walk the path that you have set before me, but in your mercy deliver me from despair.'

"Although the disappointment of not gaining my freedom was great, I realised on arriving in the West Indies that my master had not totally failed me. His instructions to the Captain of the ship were clear, 'Equiano has been a faithful servant. Make sure that you only sell him to a good master.'

"The Captain kept his word and I was sold to Mr. Robert King, a Quaker from Philadelphia. Mr. King did not beat his slaves, and was known as the best master to have in the islands.

"Working for Mr. King, I constantly prayed to God for my freedom. And as I prayed I did whatever I could to bring that day of freedom a little bit closer. My master was a merchant. With the little money that I had, I too started to trade in goods. Buying and selling at a profit, I quickly began to save the £40 that I needed to buy back my freedom. I knew that God had not forgotten me.

"Eventually the day came when I stood before my master with the money in my hand. He was shocked that I had saved such a large amount of money in such a short time, but he was a man who believed in keeping his promises. He had promised to release me on receipt of £40. So that is exactly what he did.

"Today I stand before you, able to speak these words with confidence; 'Surely God is my salvation; I will trust and not be afraid. The Lord is my strength and my song; he has become my salvation.' Today I stand before you as an African and a free man."

Equiano hesitated and looked around at his audience. He had not travelled to this city just to inform or entertain the people who had come to hear him speak. He had come with a purpose; his desire was to promote the abolition of slavery and to encourage people to support the people who were trying to change the laws of Britain.

"It is time for me to conclude the story of my life. As I do, I call upon the British government to give freedom to those who are now in bondage. May God bless those noble people who are fighting for the rights of oppressed slaves!

"Some of you, present tonight, believe that if slavery is abolished, then Britain will suffer economically. It is true that Britain has grown wealthy because of the slave trade, but I say that the abolition of slavery will result in good for everyone. Trade with Africa will increase. Industry will expand as goods are made to sell in Africa. The abolition of slavery will be in everyone's best interests.

"Today slaves are murdered, tortured and suffer the most awful abuses. The people who are doing this are going unpunished. I hope the slave trade will be abolished. And I pray that I will be alive to see it."

On the way out of the hall, Joseph's mother stopped to buy the book that Equiano had written about his life, "The Interesting Narrative of the Life of Olaudah Equiano or Gustavus Vassa, The African." The next evening Joseph sat with his family around the fireplace. His mother picked up Equiano's book and began to read out loud. As the candle flames flickered, Joseph followed the story of how an African child was taken into slavery. He felt something of Equiano's despair but also learnt of his faith and hope for freedom that kept Equiano going through many difficulties and adventures. After several nights of reading, Joseph's mother finished the book. The family were unusually quiet. Joseph, who was eleven years old, realised that he was the same age at which Equiano was taken from his family into slavery.

"I want to support the abolition of the slave trade," Joseph suddenly announced.

His father stood up, his arms behind his back.

"Yes, Joseph," his father nodded. "We will support the abolition of the slave trade. Africans are people just like us. Therefore we must do all we can to ensure that our African brothers and sisters are freed from their bondage, just like Olaudah Equiano."

At a Glance: Olaudah Equiano

Olaudah Equiano was an African who campaigned for the abolition of the slave trade. He was born in 1745, in what is now Nigeria, on the West Coast of Africa and was kidnapped as a child by slave traders. Transported to the Caribbean, Equiano was sold to a plantation owner in Virginia, North America. However, within a short time, a British navel officer, Michael Henry Pascal, bought him.

After many years working as a sailor and merchant, Equiano saved enough money to buy his freedom. He was twenty-one years old. Baptised as a Christian in his teens, Equiano joined the Methodist church after coming to a deeper understanding of God's love and forgiveness.

In 1789, Equiano published his life story. It was a best seller in Britain and America and translated into Dutch and German. Equiano hoped that his story would encourage the British Government to abolish the slave trade. However, Equiano died in 1797, whilst the slave trade was not abolished until 1807.

Fact File: Atlantic slave trade

1 The Atlantic slave trade is the name given to the capture and transportation of Africans to countries in South and North America, and the Caribbean. It is also known as the African Holocaust due to the large numbers of people who suffered and died as a result. It is estimated that 1 in 5 people, transported across the Atlantic, died before they reached their destination.

2 The first European slave traders were Portuguese. They wanted workers for their mines and sugar plantations in Brazil.

3 By the late 17th century Britain was the leading slave trading nation.

4 Most slaves at this time came from the west coast of Africa.

5 At least 12 million people were taken from Africa by European slave traders.

Faith in action

During his years at sea Olaudah could not even swim yet he survived shipwreck and war. He experienced great injustice and disappointment yet he thought deeply about spiritual questions. What does it mean to be a Christian? What does it mean to be saved? How do you know that your sins are forgiven? These were some of the questions Equiano struggled with and eventually found answers to.

At the front of his book, *The Life of Olaudah Equiano*, are some words from the Old Testament: *Surely God is my salvation; I will trust and not be afraid. The Lord, is my strength and my song; He has become my salvation. In that day you will say: Give thanks to the Lord, call on his name; Make known among the nations what he has done.. Isaiah 12: 2, 4*

Think about Equiano's life and experiences. Why did he chose these verses to put at the beginning of his book?

Talk about it

Should people apologise for the slave trade and slavery? Who should apologise? Who should be apologised to? Is it possible to apologise for something that you were not personally responsible for? Here are just three examples of apologies that have been made for slavery:

Liverpool was a major centre for the slave trade. The City Council has apologised for the city's involvement in the Slave Trade

President Kerekou of the Republic of Benin apologised for the role of African rulers in selling people into slavery

The American newspaper the Hartford Courant apologised for publishing advertisements describing run-away slaves and so helping with their capture.

Find out why some people do not agree with making these sorts of apologies. When people do apologise for the slave trade and for slavery, how do you think they can show that their apology is real and meaningful?

Make Your Voice Heard

Thank God for the abolition movement and for those who were its leaders, both free and enslaved. Thank God for ordinary men, women and children who rejected slavery and who also reject it today. Ask God to teach you from their examples. Ask him to give you the courage and strength to speak out for justice and for freedom.

Granville Sharp

JONATHAN STRONG STAGGERED ALONG THE STREET.
His head was throbbing constantly and the pain was becoming
unbearable. Occasionally the African stumbled on the cobbled
streets. Everything seemed strangely dark and often the young
man had to reach out to steady himself. Yet he knew there was no time
to lose; he must get help.

William Sharp, the King's doctor, opened the door to his office on
Mincing Lane. Already a long queue of poorly dressed people were
waiting to see him. William Sharp sighed to himself. Every morning
he gave free treatment to those who could not afford to pay a doctor,
and every morning the number of people seeking help seemed to be
growing.

Suddenly he heard a familiar voice call his name. It was his brother,
Granville.

"Quick, William! Help me with this man."

The doctor rushed out into the street. His brother was trying to stop
an African man from collapsing. Together they managed to carry the man
into the office and lay him down gently onto a bench.

"Is he dead?" Granville asked.

"No, he's breathing," the doctor replied. "But look at his head. He's got a serious injury." Immediately, William began to dress the wound. The injured man groaned with the pain and opened his eyes. "What's your name?" the doctor asked.

"Strong," came a whisper. "My name is Jonathan Strong."

At the end of the morning, Dr. William closed his office. His brother Granville was still there.

"What shall we do with Strong?" asked Granville in a quiet voice.

"Well, he can't stay here. I have to be honest. If he does not receive more medical help, he may very well die."

The two men looked at each other. From the state of Jonathan's clothes it was obvious that he had little money.

"Don't worry, William," Granville replied. "If you can get him into a hospital, I will look after the expense."

Jonathan Strong was taken to St. Bartholomew's Hospital. It would be another four and half months before he could leave. During that time Granville visited Strong and listened to his story.

"I was an enslaved man," he began. "My owner was Mr. Lisle and I was working for him in the West Indies. Then one day he announced that he was returning to Britain. He decided that I should come with him. That is how I came to be in London."

"But what about your injury. How did that happen?"

"Unfortunately, Lisle has a cruel and vicious temper. One day I did something to make him angry and he pulled out his pistol. For one moment, I thought he might shoot me. But instead he took the gun and hit me over the head. He hit me so hard that the gun broke.

"After that I was useless. I could hardly walk and soon I had a fever. Lisle kicked me out onto the street. He didn't want to look after a sick and injured man."

Sharp was shocked at what he had heard and knew that Strong would need more than medical help if he were to survive in London. Once again Granville talked to his brother.

"Sharp will need a job and a place to live, when he comes out of hospital."

William thought for a moment. "Leave it with me. I know that Mr. Brown is looking for someone to help him in his pharmacy. I'll have a word with him." So when finally Jonathan Strong left hospital, he went to live and work not far from the doctor's office. However, two years later Strong would once again find himself in danger and in need of Granville Sharp's help.

David Lisle could not believe his eyes. Quickly he darted into the door of a shop, where he would not be noticed and peered out from the shadows. Just across the road was a carriage. A footman, dressed in a smart uniform with a white wig, was opening the carriage door. He looks so much like my slave, Lisle thought to himself but then shook his head. It could not be possible. Jonathan Strong must surely be dead. Yet when Lisle looked again, he was certain. It was Jonathan Strong.

Lisle was furious. Strong had escaped and was now well enough to work. "I paid a lot of money for that man," he muttered to himself. "How dare he work for someone else. I could make some money out of him."

Lisle followed the carriage as it clattered through the narrow London streets. When it finally stopped outside the pharmacist's house, Lisle noted the address and quickly disappeared. A few days later Strong received a message.

"Come to the Inn on Fenchurch Street. I have some important news for you," the message read.

Totally unaware that he was walking into a trap, Strong went to keep his appointment. Suddenly two men grabbed him as he approached the inn. Strong fought as hard as he could, but the men were prepared. They bound his hands and dragged him away.

"Where are you taking me?" Strong pleaded. One of the men was John Ross, who ran a small prison.

"We're taking you to your master, he's got business to do with you."

Strong pleaded to be released, but Ross would not listen. Instead they dragged him up the steps of the prison, threw him into a cell and locked the door. A sea captain approached the cell, looked in and then turned away with a smile.

Strong tried to stay calm. Every evening one of the prison keepers brought him food. "What's going to happen to me?" Strong asked his jailor.

"Your master saw you and has sold you to a Jamaican planter, John Kerr. As soon as the next ship sails for the West Indies, you will be on it."

For a moment Strong was speechless. The thought of being returned to the West Indies to work as a slave was unbearable.

"Please help me!" Strong pleaded. "I'm a free man now. Lisle has no right to sell me again."

The jailor saw the despair in Strong's eyes but could not help. "I have a family to feed. I can't let you go or I'll lose my job."

"Then please let me write a letter."

The next day, the jailor brought some paper and ink to Strong. Strong had been baptised as a Christian, so the first thing that he did was to write to his godparents. The two men arrived as quickly as they could but John Ross would not let them in.

Strong managed to write another letter. This time he sent it to Granville Sharp.

"Please, please protect me. Stop me from being sold as a slave."

Sharp read the words with disbelief and made his way immediately to the prison. Once again Ross refused to let him in.

"You will let me see Jonathan Strong!" Sharp insisted as he tapped his walking stick on the ground impatiently.

"I know the lord-mayor and you will be in serious trouble if you don't let me in."Granville Sharp could look very stern when he wanted to, and finally Ross gave in. After talking to Jonathan Strong in his cell, Sharp continued to threaten the prison owner.

"Jonathan Strong has the right to a trial.You will not let anyone take him from this prison, until he appears before a magistrate!"

Sharp then went to visit the lord-mayor, Sir Robert Kite, and begged him to hear Strong's case. The day arrived for the hearing. The lawyers could not make up their minds about what to do with Jonathan Strong. So eventually the lord-mayor made the decision.

"Strong shall go free. He was kidnapped without a warrant and therefore his arrest was illegal."

The captain of the ship that was to take Strong to Jamaica was furious. He reached out and grabbed Strong, "I now claim this man as my property. He is my slave."

However Granville Sharp was prepared and moved quickly. He reached out and put his hand on the captain's shoulder.

"I charge you, in the name of the king, with assaulting Jonathan Strong. And all these people are my witnesses."

The captain looked around at the stern faces of the lawyers and the lord-mayor. With embarrassment, he let go of Jonathan Strong and marched out of the room angrily. "You will be hearing from me," he shouted back at Granville Sharp.

Jonathan Strong could now walk out of the court as a free man again, but there were many other black people in London who needed protection. Strong was not unusual. Other Africans who had claimed their freedom from slavery in England, or who had been given their freedom were always in danger of being kidnapped. Once kidnapped, these people were forced onto ships and taken back to the West Indies. Granville Sharp quickly became known as someone who was prepared to help Africans fight for their freedom. At the age of thirty-two, his life work had begun.

The first thing that Sharp had to do was to study the law. He was not a trained lawyer. In fact he had received very little education, but had studied by himself and had even learnt Greek and Hebrew in his spare time. He had wanted to be able to understand the Bible in the languages that they had been written in.

After going to court with Jonathan Strong, Granville realised that he needed to know a lot more about the law and what it really said about slavery. However, it did not take long before he found out that the law on slavery was unclear. He continued to study. Finally Sharp was certain of his facts. No one in England at that time, whether they were black or white, could be made a slave unless he or she agreed to it voluntarily. However, many lawyers did not agree with this and every court case brought by a black person had to be fought fiercely. Sharp offered help, support and advice to Africans in London who wanted to claim freedom for themselves.

John Hylas would not give up the fight to get his wife back. He remembered the day he had married Mary. They had been so happy together. Their happiness had been even greater when his master made John a free man, after the wedding. For eight years they had lived together in England until that awful day when Mary did not return to their home.

Hylas had looked everywhere for his wife, until finally he found out the truth. Before they had been married, Mary had been a slave in Barbados. Now her former owners, the Newtons, wanted her back. They had arranged for her to be kidnapped and sent back to the West Indies.

"You must take Newton to court," Granville Sharp explained to Hylas. "When you were given your freedom, your wife should also have been made free."

Hylas followed Sharp's advice and won his court case. Newton was given six months to return Mary Hylas to England.

However, Granville Sharp was furious because Newton was only made to pay Mary Hylas one shilling as compensation for her kidnap and imprisonment. The court did not treat black and white people in the same way. Sharp was determined that he would not stop until the British law gave black people their full rights to liberty and freedom in England.

What was needed was a final decision by the law courts. A decision that once and for all would declare that an African slave coming to England would become a free person. That opportunity came when James Somerset knocked on Granville Sharp's door.

"I have heard that you help people like me," Somerset started to explain. "I was kept as a slave in America. But my master, Mr. Stewart, brought me to England."

Sharp was taking careful notes of Somerset's story. Already, he had guessed how the story would continue. So many times, he had heard the same things.

"I wanted to be a free man so I ran away from my master. However, Mr. Stewart had me kidnapped. I was put on a ship ready to go to Jamaica where I was to be sold. However, I got a message to my godparents who managed to get me released. But now I have to face a court. Can you help me?"

Sharp stood and paced the room. "I will find you some good lawyers. It will be difficult but I do believe we have the law on our side. I will write to all the judges and the Prime Minister and explain why slavery is illegal in England."

The court case was to last for months. Sharp employed someone to write down everything that happened. News of the case soon spread and the courtroom was full as the arguments raged.

"No man can be held legally as a slave in England. The laws in the British colonies are different, but they do not apply to people living here," Somerset's lawyer argued. At the end of the court case, Lord Mansfield stood to make his judgment. Dressed in his full robes and white wig, he spoke clearly to the waiting crowd.

"The man James Somerset is free to go. It should be understood that a master cannot seize his slave and take him from this country against his will. Slavery is not approved by the English law."

Sitting in court that day were a group of Africans who had come to hear the verdict. That night they celebrated by dancing and cheering Lord Mansfield, for now they believed that every slave in England had a right to be free.

Granville Sharp was not in the court room for that final day. Instead he waited nervously at home. Finally the knock came to his door. To his immense relief, when he opened the door there stood James Somerset.

"I am a free man, Mr. Sharp!"

So finally in 1772, Sharp's legal work had been rewarded. The law in England now gave African people protection from being taken as slaves to other countries. However, it did not immediately end slavery in England and some people continued to ignore the law. One of these people who ignored the law was Mr. Kirkpatrick.

Olaudah Equiano did not know what to do. His close friend John Annis had been kidnapped and despite his best efforts, he had failed to find or to free him. There was still one chance of help. Equiano had heard about Granville Sharp and so decided to visit him without delay.

"So Mr. Equiano, how may I help you?"

"I have come for some advice. My friend John Annis used to work for Mr. Kirkpatrick in the West Indies. However, he managed to get his freedom and was living in London. In the spring I got a job for him working on a ship as a cook. I was the steward and we were going to sail to Turkey. However, the ship needed some repairs before it could leave England."

Sharp listened patiently as Equiano continued to describe what had happened.

"At that time Mr. Kirkpatrick began to cause problems for my friend. He wanted to take him back to St. Kitts and tried to get someone to kidnap him. But John managed to keep hidden on the ship. Eventually Mr. Kirkpatrick could wait no longer. On Easter Monday, he rowed out to us with two boats and six men.

I tried to stop them taking John, but no one else would help me. The rest of the crew just stood and watched. As soon as I could, I found out where they had taken him. But it was too late. The ship had already sailed.

I tried to get Mr. Kirkpatrick arrested. However, he simply told the judge that he did not have John Annis in his custody."

Granville Sharp gave Equiano all the help and advice he could. However, it was too late. Equiano's attempts to save his friend had failed.

John Annis was shipped back to St. Kitts in the West Indies. When he arrived back, he was tied and beaten without mercy. After the beating, he had to wear a heavy iron collar around his neck as a punishment for running away. Within a short time, Annis was dead. He had died as a result of his cruel treatment and his utter despair.

Nine years later, Olaudah Equiano once again knocked at Granville Sharp's door.

"Have you seen this letter in the newspaper?" Equiano asked. Sharp took the paper and began to read. The letter was describing a court case that was being held against the owners of a slave ship called *The Zong*.

"The letter says that the captain threw one hundred and thirty Africans alive into the sea. These men are murderers." Equiano exclaimed with anger. Sharp read the newspaper and for a moment did not know what to say.

"Thank you for bringing this to my attention, Equiano. I will find out immediately about this crime and get back to you as soon as I can."

Sharp kept his word and attended the rest of the court case. He found out what had happened aboard *The Zong*, and was horrified at what he heard. Captain Luke Collingwood was in charge of a slave ship. He had taken 440 Africans from their homes and was shipping them to Jamaica. However, right from the start things did not go well. The journey across the Atlantic took twice as long as it should have done. Then Collingwood misread his maps and missed the island of Jamaica. Already 60 people had died and many others were very sick.

The Captain knew that if the slaves died because of sickness, then the owners of the ship would receive no money. However, if they died because of danger at sea, then the owners of the ship would be able to claim insurance money for each dead slave. Captian Collingwood decided to make up a story that the ship was running out of water and that everyone on board was in danger of losing their lives. He then ordered his crew to start throwing sick men and women into the sea. After three days about 130 people had been murdered in this way.

The owners of the ship then claimed the insurance money for the dead slaves. However, the insurance company did not accept Collingwood's story. One of the crew on *The Zong*, was overcome with guilt at what had happened.

"The ship had plenty of water," he explained. "We even had water to spare when we arrived in Jamaica."

Sharp hired lawyers, took detailed notes and interviewed witnesses. However, all the judge was interested in was whether the insurance money should be paid for the dead slaves. Granville Sharp and Olaudah Equiano failed to get the men involved arrested for murder. No one was taken to court for the murder of the Africans who lost their lives on *The Zong*. The British authorities were not interested in the case.

Although, Sharp had helped black people to get their freedom in England, he knew that the rights of African people outside of the country were being totally ignored. In fact, British merchants and plantation owners did not even consider them to be people. Once African people were taken as slaves they were simply considered "property". The events that happened on *The Zong* slave ship showed that these men, women and children did not even have the right to life.

Sharp was not prepared to let the matter go. He wrote about the awful details of what had happened on *The Zong* and got the story published in newspapers. Now ordinary people could read about it for themselves. As a result more and more people began to believe that the slave trade had to be stopped. The movement to abolish the slave trade was beginning to grow. However, there was a long way to go. By 1787, Sharp, his friend Thomas Clarkson and a group of Quakers who were committed to the abolition of the slave trade decided to form a committee. The fight to end the slave trade would have to be organised if it was to succeed. The laws of Britain would have to be changed if slavery in the British colonies was to be abolished. To achieve this, the general public needed to be informed and encouraged to support abolition. And the task was urgent.

"The Bible shows us that oppression is a most terrible crime. The cries of these enslaved people will certainly reach heaven and God will bring judgment upon us," Granville warned.

Yet to stop this oppression the committee needed a spokesman in the British parliament. What Member of Parliament would be prepared to speak out against slavery? Who would be strong enough to take on the fight to change the laws of the country? Who could that man be?

At a Glance: Granville Sharp

Granville Sharp, who was born in 1735, is remembered as the "father" of the abolition movement in Britain. He started his fight against slavery by helping enslaved black people living in London claim their freedom and to fight being sent back to the West Indies by their owners.

One of these people was James Somerset. As a result of his court case in which he claimed his freedom, the judge declared that it was illegal in England to take a person by force to sell him or her as a slave.

Sharp helped to establish a colony in Africa for freed slaves. This settlement was given the name of Freetown and is today the capital of Sierra Leone.

In 1787 the Committee for the Abolition of the Slave Trade was formed. Sharp was the chairperson for this committee. William Wilberforce was to become its main spokesperson in parliament.

Fact file: Slavery in the Caribbean

1 Many people taken from Africa as slaves were sent to the Caribbean islands. Their labour was essential to run the sugar plantations that belonged to European owners. These owners could become rich through selling sugar and rum.

2 The death rate of slaves on these plantations was high. They died through overwork, accidents, disease and physical punishments. One in three of Africans, arriving in the Caribbean as slaves, died within three years.

3 There were more black people in the Caribbean than white people. This led to a constant fear of rebellion. Slaves were punished for the smallest acts of disobedience.

4 Enslaved children were also expected to work on the plantations. They pulled up weeds in fields and cut grass to feed animals. Some worked in the owner's house, helping with laundry or serving at the table. Others looked after cattle.

Faith in action

The Bible teaches us that God is a God of justice, and that those who truly believe in Him will also love justice. 'For the Lord is righteous, He loves justice; Upright men will see his face.' Psalm 11:7 'The righteous care about justice for the poor, but the wicked have no such concern.' Proverbs 29:7

Granville Sharp believed strongly in a God of justice. He also believed that God would judge nations and people who were unjust. Therefore, he tried to ensure that the law of Britain was just and fair. He fought to establish the rights of Africans to live as free people in Britain. Do we care about fairness and justice? How can we put this belief into action today?

Make your voice heard

One of the ways we can show a love of justice in our lives is to avoid discrimination. Discrimination is when we treat someone differently because of his or her race, gender, skin colour, religion or age.

Granville Sharp fought in the courts to ensure that black people had the same rights to freedom as white British people. He was fighting discrimination.

Thank God that he has made every person different. Thank Him for creating different races, languages and cultures.

Ask God to help you to celebrate and enjoy these differences. Ask him to help you to treat everyone with respect and to play your part in rejecting discrimination.

Talk About It

What types of discrimination exist today? Do you know what laws exist to fight this discrimination? Find out about these laws and what they mean in every day life.

William Wilberforce

THE STAGECOACH WAS READY TO LEAVE AND THE warm breath of the horses could be seen rising into the winter air. Pulling his thick coat around him, a short well-dressed man climbed inside. Cracking his whip, the driver urged the horses forward. It was December 1785 and the rich young man was William Wilberforce. Staring from the window, he began to catch glimpses of London life; women selling vegetables, chimney sweeps with their brushes, and beggars in rags calling out for a few coins. However, his thoughts were far away. With the noise of the wheels, came the memory of another journey - a journey that had begun to change his life.

"Come with me this winter," Wilberforce suggested to his former tutor Isaac Milner. "I'm going to France with my mother and sister. Come and keep me company. It is going to be a long trip, and I don't want to be bored!"

Wilberforce's travelling companion lived up to his expectations. The two men shared jokes and stories as the carriage trundled through the French countryside. But there were also moments of discussion and disagreement. Usually these disagreements were about religion.

"Religion is important, but I do think you can take it too far," Wilberforce explained. "Going to church is quite enough for me."

For a moment there was an uncomfortable silence as Wilberforce turned his face to look out of the window. Although he often went to church, he had little time to think about his spiritual life. There were parties to attend, clubs to visit and long evening meals to enjoy with his friends.

Milner smiled gently.

"Following Jesus Christ is not just about going to church on Sundays; it's about following Him every day of your life."

Wilberforce turned to listen. There was something about the smile on Milner's face and the kind tone of his voice that made him want to know more. The two men decided to return to England in the middle of the winter. In order to pass the time, they had agreed to read a Christian book. To his surprise, Wilberforce found it interesting.

"The best news that you can ever hear is that God sent his Son, Jesus Christ, into the world to save us," Milner read. His companion was unusually silent. Milner looked up; Wilberforce was listening carefully.

Approaching a steep hill, the carriage suddenly came to a stop. Ahead of them the rough road was covered in ice. Pulling their coats tightly around them, the two men stepped out into the ice and snow.

As the driver led the horses forward, Milner suddenly noticed that the coach was slipping. It was moving dangerously close to the edge of the road. Milner rushed forward. Putting his shoulders against the back of the carriage, he pushed with all his might. The horses snorted and heaved. Slowly the carriage began to move away from the steep drop.

At the top of the hill, the two friends laughed with relief as they climbed back into their carriage. "Let's carry on reading," Wilberforce suggested.

Milner and Wilberforce's friendship continued to deepen over the next year. Wilberforce had so many questions about the Christian faith and Milner was more than happy to answer them.

As the summer turned into autumn, Wilberforce began to get up early in the morning in order to pray. He sought God's forgiveness for his selfishness, and he sought God's strength to follow Christ in his daily life. It was these prayers that had now brought him to the point where he had to make a very important decision; a decision that Wilberforce was finding impossible to make. Deep in thought, the traveller hardly noticed the stagecoach slowing down and finally coming to a halt. The coach had arrived in East London. Even though it was cold, Wilberforce still hesitated as he approached Charles Square. Slowly he paced around the square, thinking about what he had come to say. Eventually he could delay no longer; climbing the steps, Wilberforce knocked at the home of the Rev John Newton.

The elderly church minister, John Newton, was not a stranger to Wilberforce. As a young boy he had loved to listen to Newton's sermons. However, that was many years ago, and now the small boy was a well-known Member of Parliament. As a close friend of the Prime Minister, William Pitt, Wilberforce had a great future ahead of him.

"So what has brought you to seek out an old man like me?" Newton asked with a warm smile.

Sat in front of the welcoming fire, Wilberforce began to relax.

"I want to serve God, but I am a politician. Can I really follow Christ and be a politician at the same time? Surely it would be better for me to become a church minister?"

Wilberforce paused but Newton did not reply.

Quietly Wilberforce continued.

"What should I do with my life? I have been praying about this, but the decision seems so hard to make."

John Newton nodded with understanding. He too had struggled to decide what profession to follow as a Christian. For many years he had worked as a Captain of a slave ship. Looking back, he regretted that he

55

had spent so many years transporting Africans from their homes to a life of slavery in the plantations of the West Indies. Newton could not change his past, but he hoped that in some small way he could help to change the future. Wilberforce reached into his pocket and pulled out a letter.

"Every time I make up my mind, something happens to make me feel uncertain. A few weeks ago I had decided to give up my social life and to withdraw from politics. So I wrote to the Prime Minister to tell him."

"What did he say?" asked Newton.

"He wasn't very pleased! Pitt sent me this letter saying that I would be wasting my talents. We did discuss the matter further and the Prime Minister has asked me to reconsider. So that is why I have come to you. Once again I am unsure about what to do. I knew that you would be able to give me spiritual guidance."

The old man had listened patiently. Now he turned to his visitor, to give his own opinion. Wilberforce was surprised. It was not the advice that he had expected.

"God has put you in Parliament for a reason. There you will have the chance to influence the nation and its law. I believe that God has called you to be a Member of Parliament in order to bring good to the Church and to this country. Don't throw away your talents and your opportunities."

Newton bowed his head to pray. "I will ask God to show you what He wants you to do as a politician. God will answer your prayers and He will show you the task that he has for you in Parliament."

Wilberforce left the home of John Newton with a lot to think about, but now there was peace in his mind. Over the coming months, Wilberforce continued to pray for God's guidance. Furthermore, some of his friends also felt that they knew exactly what Wilberforce should be doing with his life.

"The slave trade must be stopped!" Lady Middleton exclaimed as she firmly placed the teapot back on the table. It was a bright October morning and Sir Charles Middleton and his wife were having their breakfast.

"Of course I agree," responded her husband. "But too many people are making a living from the trade and will not want it stopped. It's not just the plantation owners who buy the slaves who would fight against abolition. There are the ship builders and the merchants; the port authorities who collect the taxes; bankers who insure the ships. So many people are involved and they have a lot of power in the country."

"But Charles, there is a growing number of people who want this trade to stop. Surely they have some power too?"

"I have to be honest with you. The only way to stop the slave trade will be to change the laws of our country. We need someone in Parliament to take up the fight."

For a moment Lady Middleton was quiet and picked up a piece of bread. She knew that any Member of Parliament who opposed the Slave Trade would make many enemies and could even lose the chance to develop his own career. Then suddenly she thought of someone who might consider such a difficult challenge.

"What about our friend, Wilberforce?"

Her husband nodded. It was a good idea. Wilberforce was a popular politician who took his position seriously.

"I'll write to him straight away and see what he has to say," Sir Middleton decided.

When the letter arrived in Hull, Wilberforce wasn't sure what to think. As he walked along the banks of the River Humber, Wilberforce watched the seabirds wading for food in the mud. Doubts filled his mind. 'Am I really the best man for the job? Do I know enough about the Slave Trade to bring it before Parliament? Do I really want to sacrifice my own ambitions?'

Yet as he turned to walk home along the narrow streets he remembered his visit to John Newton. Perhaps this was the purpose that God intended for him as a politician. Perhaps this was the task that he had been praying for. That evening Wilberforce sat to write a reply to Sir Middleton:

"I agree that the slave trade is a very important issue, but I need some more time to think about it. I'll come and visit you and we can discuss it further..."

The Prime Minister looked out of one of the windows of his large country house. The trees in the grounds were covered in young leaves. Young lambs were running around in the warm May sun. "Let's get some fresh air," Pitt suggested to his two visitors, Wilberforce, and his cousin Grenville. Deep in thought, Wilberforce walked across the park. Over the last few months, one subject had seemed to come up constantly and was now filling his mind - the abolition of the Slave Trade. Wilberforce knew that his friends were waiting for him to make a decision. They wanted him to represent the cause in Parliament, but still Wilberforce doubted whether he was the best man for the job.

Arriving at an old oak tree, Pitt sat down on one of the twisted roots. "Come and sit with me, Wilba."

With the warmth of the sunshine on his face, Wilberforce began to tell his friend all that he had been learning about the Slave Trade.

"All along the coast of Africa the Slave Trade is shutting out light and truth. Humanity and kindness mean nothing to those involved in this evil trade."

The Prime Minister was listening carefully.

"Some people are asking me to bring the matter to Parliament," Wilberforce added quietly waiting to see the response of his friend.

"Well, you have already collected a lot of information. Perhaps they are right and you should bring the abolition of the Slave Trade to Parliament," the Prime Minister responded.

Wilberforce turned to Pitt. "So you would support me?"

"Yes, I will. But it will be a long, hard fight. Think about it, my friend. But don't take too long making up your mind. The movement to end the slave trade must move forward, and move forward quickly."

Wilberforce knew that Pitt was right. The task would be enormous. Changing the law in England could be long and difficult. However, on that quiet afternoon as a gentle breeze rustled the leaves on the tree, Wilberforce knew that the time had come to make a decision.

Some months later, Wilberforce was to pick up his quill and write confidently in his diary, "God Almighty has set me two great objectives, the suppression of the Slave Trade and the improvement of conditions within society." At the age of twenty eight, William Wilberforce finally knew for certain what God wanted him to do with the rest of his life.

Wilberforce welcomed the tall visitor into his study. Papers and pamphlets were littered all across the desk. A half-written letter lay waiting to be finished. The tired-looking visitor placed a heavy bag onto the floor and sat down.

"Well Clarkson, how was the trip?"

Thomas Clarkson hesitated for a moment. For the last few months, he had been visiting the seaports of Bristol and Liverpool. His task was to collect as much evidence as he could about the Slave Trade so that it could be presented to Parliament. Clarkson had collected so many facts that it was difficult to know where to begin.

In careful detail, Clarkson began to describe the slave ships he had visited. He gave facts about the large numbers of sailors who died working on them. From interviews with captains, he described the cruelty experienced by the slaves.

Finally, he opened his bag and took out three metal objects.

Wilberforce lent forward, picked one of them up and turned it in his hand. It was a metal leg chain.

"This is a thumb-screw used to punish slaves," Clarkson continued as he picked up the second object. "And this piece of metal is placed inside a slave's mouth so that he can be force fed if he refuses to eat."

"Where did you get these things?" Wilberforce asked amazed.

"They were on sale in a shop in Liverpool."

Clarkson sat back in his chair, his long legs stretched out in front of him. Wilberforce had been making careful notes of everything his friend had said. He now put down his quill.

"This is the sort of evidence that I need to proceed. I can now inform Parliament of my intentions to seek the abolition of the Slave Trade."

However, both men knew that this would be just the beginning of hours, days and months of careful research. Thomas Clarkson travelled throughout the country. Wilberforce interviewed people, read reports and wrote down all the information he could find.

Over a year later, everything was ready. In May 1789 Wilberforce stood to give his speech to parliament.

"We are all guilty of supporting the Slave Trade," Wilberforce spoke in a calm voice. "I have not come to make accusations but to present evidence that will show you the true nature of this trade."

Whatever people thought of the Slave Trade there was one fact that no one could argue about and that was the high death rate amongst slaves taken from Africa to the West Indies. Wilberforce knew that this was the most important piece of evidence against the slave trade:

"Fifty percent of Africans transported in the trade end up dead. They die as they wait on board ship in the rivers and on the coastlines of Africa. They die in the voyage across the sea and they die on arrival as they adjust to the new conditions in the West Indies. The number of deaths speaks for itself."

After talking for more than three hours, Wilberforce came to his conclusion. "A trade based on such evil and carried out with such cruelty must be abolished. I am determined that I will not rest until I have achieved its abolition."

Many of the men, listening to Wilberforce were moved by his speech. They knew that what he was saying was true. However, they had other concerns. Some of them feared that the abolition of the slave trade would bring economic ruin. Others benefited personally from the slave trade. So that night, Parliament decided not to take any action. The politicians insisted that they needed more information.

However, just as he had promised, Wilberforce did not give up. Year after year, he stood in front of Parliament to present a Bill so that a law could be made to abolish the slave trade. Time and time again, politicians voted against it. Sometimes this was due to world events, outside of Wilberforce's control.

One evening in August 1791, on the island of San Domingo in the West Indies, groups of slaves were meeting as the sun disappeared. "We will be free!" they vowed.

Collecting what weapons they could, large numbers of slaves began to move towards the houses of their masters. With flaming torches they set light to the plantations. There was to be no escape for many slave-owning families. Men, women and children were murdered. Many thousands of slaves were also killed in the uprising. The news spread quickly to the other West Indian islands and back to Britain.

Wilberforce put down his newspaper. He knew what people were saying about him. The cartoons in the newspaper with their cruel jokes made it quite clear. "Wilberforce is to blame for the thousands of dead on San Domingo. Promising slaves freedom will only lead to death and destruction," came the message.

Wilberforce bowed his head. This would lead to more opposition, and more delays. However, Wilberforce believed that it was every slave's right to be free. Whatever the newspapers said, Wilberforce would continue the fight to end the slave trade.

Sometimes, unexpected factors prevented the Bill being passed. In 1796 Wilberforce walked confidently into the Houses of Parliament. Wilberforce knew that this time he could win the vote, as enough politicians had promised to support him. However, it was nearly Easter and some of Wilberforce's supporters had already left London to go to their country homes. Furthermore, that night a new opera had opened. At least 5 of his supporters had decided to attend. As Wilberforce stood to give his speech he looked around. The benches seemed to be a little emptier than he had hoped. When the results of the vote were made known, his worse fears were realised. He had lost the vote by only 4. Another year was wasted. Another opportunity had gone.

Wilberforce could not believe what had happened. If only his supporters had all attended parliament instead of going to the opera, the Bill would have been passed. He sat down, feeling suddenly very unwell. Back home, he collapsed, exhausted from all his work and disappointments.

Once again, John Newton encouraged his friend:

"The God you serve will preserve and deliver you. Remember the story of Daniel in the lion's den. He trusted God and God delivered him. You, too, are facing many enemies. Follow Daniel's example and stay faithful to the task that God has given you."

Eleven more years would pass before the day came when Wilberforce finally saw Parliament agree to abolish the Slave Trade.

With his head in his hands, Wilberforce sat in Parliament and listened to the speeches supporting the end of the Slave Trade. Then one by one the politicians began to stand up and turn towards Wilberforce. Then they began to cheer and to shout. After all these years, his work had finally been rewarded. Tears streamed down his face as his feelings simply overwhelmed him. That day in February 1807, the slave trade was finally made illegal. However, Wilberforce's work was not finished. His next task was to campaign for the complete end of slavery and the freeing of all slaves. This he did until 1825, when he had to retire because of ill health. However, by this time other younger politicians had taken up the fight.

It was 1833 and Wilberforce was old and frail. His eyesight was so bad that he could no longer read for himself. Yet he continued to encourage and support those who were continuing the fight against slavery. "Our Motto must be to keep on persevering and not to give up. Eventually God will give us success," he had written to one of his friends.

"Wilba?" Barbara Wilberforce spoke gently to her husband as he lay resting on the couch.

"Tom Macaulay has come straight from Parliament to talk to you." Opening his eyes, Wilberforce peered toward the door.

"Now don't talk too long," Barbara tried to instruct the visitor, but her husband raised his hand.

"I have waited a long time for this day, my dear. Please don't worry about me." The politician drew up a chair beside the sick man.

"Finally God has answered our prayers." Tom Macaulay began to describe what had happened in Parliament. "The Bill to abolish slavery has been passed. And Parliament has agreed to pay slave owners compensation for freeing their slaves."

Suddenly Wilberforce felt a lot younger. His excitement gave him new strength. Sitting upright, he grasped Tom's hand. "Thank God for this wonderful news. I never thought I would live to see the day when England would be willing to pay millions of pounds to end slavery."

Three days later, William Wilberforce died.

At a Glance: William Wilberforce

William Wilberforce, born in Hull in 1759, became the spokesman for the abolition movement in the British parliament. In 1785 he had become an Evangelical Christian and dedicated his political life to abolishing slavery and reforming society. He presented his first bill to abolish the slave trade in 1791, when it was easily defeated. He continued to present bills to abolish the slave trade until 1807, when the Abolition of the Slave Trade bill finally became law. Wilberforce then campaigned for the gradual end of slavery itself.

He retired as a Member of Parliament in 1825, but continued to support the abolition movement. Wilberforce died in July 1833. One month later, Parliament passed the Slavery Abolition Act.

Fact file: The abolition of the Atlantic slave trade

1 The first European country to ban the slave trade was Denmark in 1792.

2 Despite the protests of plantation owners, the slave trade was banned by Britain in 1807. The Act imposed a fine of £100 for every slave found aboard a British ship.

3 The British Government decided to try to stop other countries from transporting slaves by sea. From 1815, the British Royal Navy patrolled the coasts of Africa to stop ships carrying Africans into slavery.

4 Other countries such as USA, Spain, Portugal and France also banned the slave trade. Brazil continued to trade in enslaved people until Britain took military action against its coast in 1851.

5 However, illegal trading still continued until Brazil banned slavery in 1888. It is estimated that at least 4 million Africans were taken to Brazil as slaves.

Faith in action

It is difficult to understand why it took so long to abolish the slave trade or how difficult it was to change people's attitudes. However, Wilberforce and his friends understood that the campaign against slavery would not be won overnight. It would take total dedication and commitment.

John Wesley, an important Christian leader, was reading Olaudah Equiano's book in 1791. As he read about the injustices experienced by African slaves, he thought about Wilberforce and wrote a letter to encourage him: *'Unless God has raised you up for the purpose of opposing this scandal ... you will be worn out by the opposition of men and devils. But if God be for you, who can be against you? Oh be not weary of well doing! Go on, in the name of God and in the power of his might...'* Or in more modern language... You are facing an impossible job! Don't give up. If you are doing God's will, then you will succeed. Trust God and let Him give you the strength you need. William Wilberforce did trust God and never gave up the fight against slavery.

Talk about it

Many people disagreed with Wilberforce and the abolition movement. Here are just a few of the arguments that supporters of the slave trade used:

It is impossible to run the plantations in the West Indies without slaves

The economy of Britain depends on slave labour

Africans have a better life living as slaves than living as free people in Africa.

Africans are not the same as Europeans

It is acceptable to own slaves as long as you treat them well

English workers in industry have a worse life than African slaves

Wilberforce is more concerned about injustice overseas than at home

Wilberforce should keep his faith and Christian beliefs private.

Wilberforce had to argue against people who said these sorts of things. What do you think he may have said to these people who disagreed with him?

Make your voice heard

In 2007, it will be 200 years since the abolition of the slave trade. We will be reminded that when people work together, society can be changed for the better. Slavery in the past and today will be explained and people will be encouraged to fight against modern day slavery. You can help to remember the abolition of the slave trade by: Watching TV programmes that explain this event; Joining in with remembrance activities in your area; Visiting the websites that promote this event. Pray to God for those people and organisations who are fighting slavery today.

Elizabeth Heyrick

 "JOHN SMITH IS DEAD." ELIZABETH HEYRICK READ THE newspaper report carefully, folded it up and walked towards the window. In silence she thought about the Methodist missionary who had died in a prison cell in the British colony of Demerara. Then she began to think about the other people who had died in Demerara during the year of 1823. These people had been slaves working on British owned plantations. They had been killed for demanding their right to be treated as human beings and for their right to be free. The thought of these deaths filled her with anger.

"I am fed up with hearing that slavery should be abolished slowly. It is time to act. Slaves should be freed immediately," she thought to herself.

John Smith was dismayed at what he saw on the plantations of Demerara. He had arrived as a missionary in 1817, and yet he could not get used to what he saw and heard. Every morning he awoke to the sound of the whip cracking as enslaved men and women made their way to the fields.

The members of his chapel complained to him about their punishments. The authorities complained to him about his missionary work.

"If you ever teach a slave to read, I will deport you from Demerara," the Governor had threatened him.

During 1823 a rumour began to spread from plantation to plantation. "The King has given us our freedom, but the Governor of the colony and our masters are refusing to tell us," people whispered to each other as they cut the sugar cane.

This was in fact not true. All that had happened was that the British government had passed some laws to try to improve the conditions on the plantations. Plantation managers were no longer allowed to flog women. One group of men, however, began to meet together to plan how they could claim their right to freedom. One of them, called Quamina, was a senior deacon at Rev. Smith's chapel.

For years Quamina had worked faithfully on the plantation of his owner. He had even managed to have a family life, despite the fact that slaves were not allowed to legally marry. For nearly twenty years, Quamina had lived with Peggy as his wife. He loved Peggy dearly and was heart broken when she fell ill. He knew that his wife was dying and had only a few hours to live. However, Quamina was not allowed to stay with Peggy through her last hours. Instead he was forced to go to work.

By the time he returned at the end of the day, Peggy was dead. Yet despite being treated in this way, Quamina did not want to use violence against the white plantation owners and workers.

"We must not murder anyone when we claim our freedom," Quamina stated.

"Rather we should go on strike. If we refuse to work, they will have to listen to us."

"Yes, but even if we strike we should still get some guns to protect ourselves."

Quamina understood what was being said. What would they do if the plantation owners did not listen? The white authorities had plenty of guns and would not be afraid to use them. How could the protesters protect themselves? Yet still he would not accept the use of guns.

"I do not believe it is right to take another man's life. Only God can give life, and only God should take it away. Let me talk to Rev. Smith. He will know what to do," suggested Quamina.

The Rev. Smith sat and listened carefully to Quamina. He was not surprised at the planned strike. There had been rumours of such a thing for a long time.

"Quamina, one day there will be freedom for everyone in Demerara, but you must be patient. Rebellion will only lead to people's death."

Yet despite the missionary's warning, the rebellion began on 18th August. It spread quickly until at least 11,000 had joined the protest. However, the people who joined the rebellion did not try to murder their white masters. Instead the rebels captured them and put them in stocks so that they would understand what it was like to be punished in that way.

Immediately British troops and local armed forces immediately began to attack the groups of protesting people. On the third day, 2,000 slaves stood and faced the troops of Colonel Leahy. The slaves refused to surrender and so the troops began to fire. The result was a massacre. By the end of the day, as least 200 enslaved men and women lay dead in the cotton fields and along the roads. The Rev. Smith was arrested and put on trial. He was accused of encouraging slaves to rebel. The court found him guilty and sentenced him to be hung.

During the court case Smith had managed to write a message on a piece of paper and get it smuggled out to his friends. The message was simply "2 Corinthians 4:8-9". Smith wanted to show his friends that despite his situation he was not afraid. The Bible verses read:

"We are hard pressed on every side, but not crushed; perplexed, but not in despair; persecuted, but not abandoned; stuck down but not destroyed."

John Smith lay in his prison cell. It was a dark, hot dungeon. Under the floorboards was a pool of stinking water. Smith began to grow weaker. His cough kept him awake at night and now he found that he was coughing up blood.

Back in England, the King agreed to pardon the missionary and set him free. However, the news never reached him. In February 1824 John Smith died.

The news of Rev. Smith's death quickly reached people living in Britain. Many people were dismayed at the news and shocked at the violence and punishments used against the people who had taken part in the uprising. Elizabeth Heyrick was one of these people who were deeply distressed at the death of enslaved men and women in Demerara.

"People call John Smith a Christian martyr. But I say that those people who died for their freedom should also be called Christian martyrs," she exclaimed to her friend, Susanna Watts.

In the previous year, British abolitionists had set up the Society for the Gradual Abolition of Slavery. Heyrick disagreed with the title.

"What these enslaved people need is immediate abolition. They need their freedom now!" Heyrick sighed.

Together Watts and Heyrick discussed what they could do about this situation. They quickly came up with a plan.

"Let's organise a boycott of sugar," Watts suggested.

"Yes, that's a great idea," Heyrick agreed "If people stop buying sugar that has been produced by slaves, then the plantations in the West Indies will fail. We certainly can't wait around for our politicians to sort the situation out. We'll be waiting for ever!"

Elizabeth Heyrick already had experience in trying to change the way that society worked, and in trying to change people's lives for the better.

As a young woman she had been married for eight years, but then her husband had died. Heyrick was devastated. For a while she moved back to live with her family and did not know what to do with her life. She prayed to God and asked him to guide her. Heyrick became a Quaker and dedicated her life to serving God.

The first thing that she did was to start a school and become a teacher. Yet that was not enough for her. She began to help poor Irish people who had come to England to work. Not content with helping these poor families, she also wanted to know what it was like to live like they did. She used to go and live in a simple cottage, eating only the basic of foods so that she understood what it was like to be hungry.

Heyrick also started to visit people in prison. At that time, prisons were filthy, crowded places. There were no beds or washing basins for cleaning clothes. Disease spread easily amongst the prisoners. Sometimes prisoners were forced to stay in prison after their sentences had finished, because they could not afford to pay the prison fees. Heyrick tried to help some of these prisoners by paying their fees.

Heyrick had even tried to stop bull baiting. This was a cruel but popular sport. Dogs were trained to grab bulls by their nose and then not to let go. The bulls were tormented and the dogs were often tossed to their deaths. Heyrick protested and wrote leaflets against it. On one occasion she actually stole the bull that was going to be used and hid it in a cottage. However, at that time women were expected to live a quiet life devoted to their families. They were certainly not supposed to be involved in political issues or to do such things as organising boycotts. However Heyrick was prepared for the criticism and so the sugar boycott began in her hometown of Leicester.

Elizabeth Heyrick and her friend, Susanna, knocked on the first door of a row of poorly built cottages. Finally a woman, holding a baby, opened the door.

"Please excuse us, but we have come to ask you to think about the sugar that you use. Do you know that if you buy sugar from the West Indies it will have been produced by enslaved people?"

The woman nodded her head. "Yes, I know that, but we like our sugar. And what can we do about the slaves? We don't own them!"

"We may not own slaves, but when we buy goods produced by slaves we are helping the plantation owners. We must show that we care about our enslaved brothers and sisters. You can do this by buying sugar that has been produced in other parts of the world where people are paid to work in the sugar plantations. Please think about changing your sugar," Watts replied.

"That's all very well but we are a poor family. West Indian sugar is the cheapest."

"I know this is true. But slavery is a sin against God. We all have a responsibility to help end it, whatever the cost," Heyrick answered.

The woman at the door smiled at her visitors. "I will think about it," she promised.

As the people in Leicester listened to the arguments of two women, many of them agreed. They began to avoid sugar grown by enslaved people and even stopped shopping from grocers who sold sugar from the West Indies. Across the country other women joined the protest. They spread the message that every individual should do something to help bring the end to slavery.

However, Heyrick was not satisfied. She wanted to get her message to more people. The only way to do this was to write booklets, so this is what she did. Heyrick wrote a booklet demanding the immediate end of slavery and published it with the title, "Immediate not Gradual Abolition". Her pamphlet certainly made an impact. One of the effects was that she upset some of the men who were leading the Anti Slavery Society. They were trying to get the government to change the law and thought that their best chance was to ask for slavery to be ended gradually. When Heyrick's pamphlet was published, even William Wilberforce was upset. This was not surprising as the pamphlet criticised politicians!

Heyrick may have upset some of the male leaders of the abolition movement, however, many women agreed with what she had written and what she was trying to do. The time had come for women to form their own groups to campaign against slavery. Elizabeth Heyrick helped to form the first women's anti-slavery society in Britain in 1825. This group became known as the Female Society for Birmingham and Elizabeth Heyrick looked after the Society's money.

After Birmingham, women in other towns began to form groups. Soon there was a network across the country of women who were prepared to knock on doors, collect signatures for petitions and give money to help people and organisations fighting slavery. Many of these women's groups read Heyrick's pamphlets in their meetings and used her writing to spread the message that slavery had to be abolished immediately.

Heyrick was a woman who spoke out for freedom at a time when women were not even allowed to vote. She believed that justice and liberty were more important than what people thought about her. The most important thing that Heyrick did was to demand that slavery be abolished immediately rather than it being a slow, gradual process. To achieve this aim, she asked ordinary men, women and children to help with the task. She believed that God demanded a total end to slavery and therefore further delay was totally unacceptable.

Back in Demerara, despite so many people having been killed or punished cruelly, the enslaved people of that colony continued to fight for their freedom in many different ways. Here is a list of some of the things that people were punished for doing in 1828: hitting the manager, biting the manager, refusing to work, not finishing a days work, quitting the field, holding secret meetings at night, helping runaways, having gunpowder, neglect of duty. In the chapels, Christians continued to pray. Surely freedom was not far away.

At a Glance: Elizabeth Heyrick

In 1824 Elizabeth Heyrick published a pamphlet *Immediate not Gradual Abolition*. She argued that only a total and immediate end to slavery was acceptable. As a Quaker, she believed that this was what God demanded.

Heyrick organised women's anti-slavery groups in Britain to campaign for the immediate end to slavery. Through her efforts the main Anti-Slavery Society finally agreed to drop the words "gradual abolition" from its title and to fully support the campaign for immediate abolition.

Heyrick's pamphlets were also read in America where her writing encouraged other women to take a more active role in campaigning against slavery. Elizabeth Heyrick died in 1831. She never saw the results of her work.

Fact file - Slave Rebellions

1 Slave rebellions included committing suicide, running away, and refusing to work hard. Groups of slaves rebelled and fought for their freedom. This happened in Africa, on slave ships and in the countries that they were taken to. In the USA, 250 attempted uprisings took place involving 10 or more people.

2 In August 1791, in San Domingo, a slave rebellion lead to thirteen years of struggle. In 1804 the country became independent and was renamed Haiti.

3 People who supported slavery often claimed that slaves were contented with their lives. Slave rebellions showed that this was a lie.

4 Many of the leaders of The 1823 Demerara Slave Uprising had been born as slaves and had never known freedom. This showed that all slaves, born in Africa or born into slavery, longed to be free. Christian people took part. They helped to prevent the killing of white people during the rebellion. The cruel behaviour of the white authorities, compared to the behaviour of those rebelling, caused an outcry in Britain, and helped to bring about the abolition of slavery.

Faith behind the action

One symbol of the abolition movement was designed by potter, Josiah Wedgwood. It showed an African man in chains with the words: Am I not a man and a brother? The women's anti-slavery groups, had their own symbol. It showed a woman in chains asking the question: Am I not a woman and a sister?

Heyrick believed that to enslave a fellow human being was to enslave a brother or a sister, and was a sin against God. God has created each individual person. We should respect others and their right to freedom and to justice.

Talk about it

Elizabeth Heyrick believed that slaves should be compensated. When Britain abolished slavery, it compensated the slave-owners but not the slaves.

Today many people are demanding that businesses and Western governments should make reparations for the slave trade. This involves admitting the wrongs of the past and paying compensation. Reparations may mean *Compensation for African countries and Compensation for the descendents of slaves.*

Arguments for reparations: *The slave trade was a crime against humanity; People are still experiencing the negative effects of slavery today; Other groups of people have received reparations for wrongs in the past.*

Arguments against reparations: *It is too late; It is difficult to find out who is a genuine descendant of a slave; Western governments were not totally responsible; Africans and Arab countries also took part in the slave trade.*

What do you think?"

Make your voice heard

People made their voices heard when protesting against slavery by boycotting goods that were produced by slaves. Elizabeth Heyrick encouraged people not to buy sugar that had been produced in the West Indies. Today when we buy "Fair trade" goods such as bananas and chocolate, we are showing that we want farmers to be paid a fair price for their goods, wherever they live in the world. Do you buy "Fair trade" chocolate or other goods? Where do you buy your clothes? To find out more about slavery and fair trade go to the web page: www.antislavery.org/homepage/campaign/slavetradevfairtrade.pdf

Elizabeth believed that one of the main causes of slavery was greed. Greed puts money first, and people second. The opposite of greed is generosity. Thank God for all the things that you have in your life such as food, clothing and shelter. Ask him to make you a generous person who is willing to share and to help others.

Samuel Sharpe

 THE PLANTATION OWNERS IN JAMAICA WERE furious. "What do these abolitionists know about our slaves? How dare they demand the end of slavery? How could we possibly grow sugar without the use of slaves? Wilberforce spreads such lies about what happens here!"

The authorities in Jamaica were nervous. Every year hundreds of slaves attempted to escape. Most of these people were recaptured, however there were always some who simply disappeared into the hills. "What will happen if the slaves rebel? Will they kill all the white people on the island? Will there be enough soldiers to protect everyone? What do the missionaries teach the slaves? Are they encouraging slaves to rebel?"

Enslaved people living in Jamaica were angry. "Why are we still being kept as slaves? Why is it taking so long to end our misery? When will the abolition of slavery come? Can we trust our owners to be honest with us?" Samuel Sharpe was one of these people who could not understand why freedom was taking so long to come. He certainly did not trust the plantation owners and slowly he was losing patience.

Sam Sharpe was not a plantation worker. Instead he lived in the town with his owner, who had taught him to read. His duties were to work in the house. Intelligent and hard working, Sharpe's owner trusted him and allowed him considerable freedom.

One of the freedoms that he had was to go to church. Sam Sharpe also had his own Bible that he loved to read and study for himself. To show his faith in Jesus Christ, Sharpe was baptised. He became a member of the Baptist Missionary Chapel in Montego Bay. The minister in charge of the chapel was Thomas Burchell.

Thomas Burchell had to be careful about what he said to his congregation. As a member of the Baptist Missionary Society, he was not allowed to publicly speak out against slavery. However, Burchell did not agree with slavery and within his chapel everyone, both free and enslaved, were treated the same.

"Christ came to save everyone," he preached. "And when Christ makes us free from our sins, we are free indeed."

One part of missionary work was to open schools where free and enslaved people were taught to read and write. Enslaved people were also allowed to become church leaders and deacons. Sharpe was one of those leaders. As a deacon of the chapel in Montego Bay, it was one of his responsibilities to teach other members of the church. It was not always possible for enslaved people to attend church. So Sam Sharpe went out to visit his fellow Christians on the plantations around the bay, where they worked. His owner allowed him time for these church responsibilities. With his Bible in his hand, Sharpe went to teach and to pray with people. Sometimes they met in groups in the fields. Sometimes they met in small groups in people's homes.

Through these visits, Sharpe knew all about the life of enslaved people on the sugar plantations of Jamaica. The rich soil and large amounts of rain produced good quality sugar. Yet the work needed to grow this sugar was harsh, unpleasant and never ending.

Growing and harvesting sugar cane was extremely hard work. People working in the fields had to plant the sugar cane in holes, dug by hand. When the harvest was ready it had to be carried to the mill. At the mill the sugar cane was put through a machine so that all the juice of the sugar came out. This juice was then simmered and turned into sugar in the boiling house.

Harvest time was exhausting work because the juice in the sugar cane could not be left as it went bad. In the hot sun, men and women cut the cane with machetes. In the mills and boiling houses many labourers were forced to work twelve hours at a time. Sometimes people were so tired, that they dozed off and were injured by the machinery or by the boiling sugar syrup. Many of the owners of these plantations did not live in Jamaica. White managers ran their plantations. These managers used to choose enslaved men to work as supervisors. These men were called "drivers".

A driver was responsible for making the other slaves work and responsible for looking after the estate. As a sign of their position, these men carried with them a long, thick whip with a short handle. A crack of these whips sounded like a gunshot and was used to let people know that it was time to go to the fields to work. These whips were also used to punish people who did not work hard enough.

During 1831, people on the estates were not only unhappy about their working conditions, they were also unhappy because many felt that the authorities on the island were deceiving them. Rumours were everywhere.

"Have you heard, the "free paper" has arrived from England," people whispered amongst themselves. This "free paper" was supposed to be a statement from the British government that all slaves were to be set free.

"Then why haven't we been told about it?" others asked.

"It's our masters. They are keeping it a secret. They don't want us to be free and they are ignoring the laws from Britain," came the reply.

The missionaries on the island tried to tell their congregations that this rumour was false.

"There is no "free paper". Instead you need to be patient," the missionaries tried to explain. "Freedom will come, but you will need to continue to wait."

Some people believed their pastors. Other people longed for freedom so much that they could not accept what they were being told. One of these people was Samuel Sharpe. He began to think of a plan to force the plantation owners to give people their freedom.

Sharpe chose Christmas as the time to take action. Enslaved people were allowed three days holiday for Christmas. On the plantations, people were given very little time off. Sunday was the only day they did not work for their owners. However on these days, they had to work on their own vegetable gardens in order to have enough to eat. This was also the day that they could go to market to sell their produce and so earn some money for themselves. So the three days at Christmas were always a special time.

"We will start our protest after the Christmas holiday," Sharpe informed a group of head drivers who had come to meet him. "We will refuse to work any more unless we are paid."

"Yes, but how will we actually do this?" asked one of the men.

Someone else put forward an idea. "We will go and take our orders from our manager as usual after Christmas. Then we will crack our whips to call people to come to work. However, no one should come, instead they should stay at home. This is how we should organise our protest."

However another of the drivers called Johnstone disagreed. "That won't work! As soon as some of the women see the driver in the field, they will be too frightened and will go to the fields to work."

Johnstone paused for a moment. "I think that the best thing to do is to go to the estate manager and tell him outright that people know that they are free and therefore they will no longer work without some sort of payment."

In his mind, Johnstone continued to imagine what would happen next. "Now by the time I tell him this, the manager will be calling for his horse and will be on his way to the Bay to say that we are rebelling. But we won't let him go! Instead we will take away his horse and his gun and will try to explain the situation to him. We will tell him that we are not rebelling, but we won't work without payment. We have worked long enough for nothing!"

Everyone else in the meeting nodded his head in agreement. It seemed so straightforward. Sharpe and his friends had agreed a plan. Now they began to spread the word from person to person, from plantation to plantation.

On Christmas day, Sharpe and some of the other leaders of the protest went to church as usual. Afterwards they met to have breakfast together. The discussion about the strike was still continuing. Thomas Williams one of the church leaders had tried to warn them not to strike,

"If freedom has really come, we will get it quietly not by striking."

But Sharpe would not change his mind.

"I have read it in a newspaper. We are free already and I have taken an oath not to work after Christmas until I am paid."

Yet Sharpe's plan for a peaceful protest could never succeed. Not all the slaves agreed with him or wanted to take part in his protest. Other people had different ideas and wanted to destroy the plantations where they worked or punish the managers for their harsh treatment.

Furthermore, the plantation managers would never listen to their workers or consider their requests. Some managers had even said that if Britain granted their slaves freedom, then they would kill them first. One rumour was that the plantation owners were going to shoot all the men and keep the women and children as slaves.

Two days after Christmas the sun had hardly set when fires could be seen dotted around the hills surrounding Montego Bay. One after another, new fires quickly lit up the hillsides. The red of the fires was reflected off the dark night sky until it became one sheet of flames. In the town the people watched in horror. As each new fire began, they could tell which plantation was being destroyed.

The peaceful protest had quickly turned to violence. People were burning the sugar fields and the warehouses. Over 200 plantations were damaged causing over a million pounds of damage.

However, the authorities were prepared. They already knew that there was going to be trouble after Christmas. Most white women and children had left their estates and moved into the town. British troops and local armed forces were ready to fight against the rebelling people. They began to attack the people on the plantations who were refusing to work. The rebels who had guns tried to fight back. About 200 slaves and fourteen white people died as a result of the fighting.

Sharpe moved around the countryside trying to help wherever he was called. Yet there was so much confusion that he could see that it was a hopeless situation. People were being shot and their homes and gardens destroyed. There was too much suffering. Sharpe handed himself over to the authorities and was put in jail.

Within a couple of weeks the authorities had taken control again and the rebellion had finally ended by the beginning of February. The plantation managers and the local authorities were quick to punish the communities that had supported the rebellion. About 310 rebels were shot or hung.

A further 285 were sentenced to other punishments including flogging.

The Jamaican authorities were also quick to take their revenge against the missionaries. Many of the leaders of the rebellion were church deacons. Surely the missionaries must have encouraged them to rebel. Two missionaries were arrested, including the Baptist missionary, William Knibb. When Thomas Burchill arrived back in Jamaica, after having been in Britain, he too, was arrested. Furious with the missionaries, mobs of armed men went through the towns, destroying the chapels and the property of the missionary societies. Nearly everything belonging to the Baptist Missionary Society was destroyed.

Finally, the trial of the three missionaries began. When it came to Burchill's trial some of the witnesses refused to cooperate with the authorities. Susan Mackenzie, an enslaved woman and member of his church, was called to give evidence against him. She refused.

"Mr. Burchill has done nothing wrong. He did not tell people to rebel against their owners," she claimed. As a punishment, Susan Mackenzie was taken and flogged. Her punishment was so bad that she was never able to walk properly again.

Other people were forced to give evidence against the remaining missionaries. However, they also found their own way to show support for the church ministers. The evidence they gave did not make sense. It was clear to the court that the evidence was false and so they had no choice but to release the missionaries.

Samuel Sharpe, however, was not released. He was sentenced to death. As Sharpe sat in his prison cell, various people came to visit him. Everyone wanted to ask him why had the slaves rebelled?

"Were you treated badly by your master?"

"No, personally, I was not treated badly."

Calmly, Sharpe tried to explain to one of the missionaries that had been sent to question him.

"I have learnt by reading my Bible that whites have no more right to hold black people in slavery than black people have to make white people slaves."

"Do you have anything you want forgiveness for?" the missionary asked.

Sharpe paused and thought for a moment.

"I am sorry that so many people have died as a result of my actions. I am also sorry that so much property has been destroyed. But I have done nothing wrong in demanding my freedom. For this I will not apologise."

The day of his execution was set for May 23rd. As he waited to be hung, his words were clear, "I would rather die upon yonder gallows than live in slavery."

Shortly after Sharpe's execution, William Knibb was sailing into the port of Liverpool in England. He had been sent by the church in Jamaica with the task of making people in Britain aware of what was happening in their country. As the ship drew into the harbour, William Knibb made a vow.

"I will see the end of slavery. I will never rest, day or night, until I see it destroyed totally," he promised.

First he had to persuade the Committee of the Baptist Missionary Society to allow him to tour the country to campaign against slavery. However, William Knibb was not going to accept a "no" to his request.

"Myself, my wife and children are totally dependent on the Baptist Mission. We have come to this country without a penny to support ourselves. However, if you will not allow me to campaign against slavery I will still continue. Even if I have to walk through this country barefoot, I will let the Christians in England know what their brothers and sisters in Jamaica are suffering."

The committee considered his request. They were in agreement and within days they had given Knibb an opportunity to talk to the annual meeting of the missionary society.

The hall was packed with hundreds of people. As Knibb stood and looked out at the vast crowd, he knew that he was about to make the most important speech of his life.

"I am here to speak for the 20,000 Baptists in Jamaica, who have no place to worship, no rest on a Sunday, no houses of prayer. Many of these 20,000 people will be flogged every time they are caught praying." Knibb continued to describe the condition of the slaves in Jamaica.

"I have seen a child flogged on Macclesfield Estate. Catherine Williams was beaten and kept in a dungeon, because she refused to live with a white man who was not her husband. I have seen people whipped so badly that their wounds had not healed after a month. William Black of King's Valley estate, is just one of these men."

Knibb picked up a metal collar that was spiked and was used to punish slaves. People booed and hissed as he raised it so that all could see. "I call upon children, parents and Christians on behalf of people such as Catherine Williams and William Black to support the abolition of slavery. I call for freedom."

As Knibb made his speeches, he also spoke up to support Samuel Sharpe. "If Sharpe had been a European man fighting for his freedom, then the people of England would have built a memorial to him."

Whilst Knibb was convincing the general public that the enslaved people of Jamaica should no longer be kept in slavery, the government was finally accepting that there was no longer any option but to abolish slavery.

After the slave revolt in Demerara and now the slave revolt in Jamaica, it was obvious that enslaved people in the British West Indies were no longer going to accept their lack of freedom. Slave revolts were too costly for the British government. It was impossible to send enough soldiers to keep the peace. If enslaved people were not given their freedom, then they would take it for themselves.

A week after the death of Samuel Sharpe, the British Government set up a committee. It's job was to find a way to bring about the end to slavery. Quietly behind the scenes, William Knibb was also talking to politicians and reporting to this government committee. To one politician he gave this warning,

"After what has happened in Jamaica, the people are no longer afraid of the punishments they have seen. They now consider death to be better than slavery and are burning with revenge for their friends and relations. The present state of affairs cannot go on much longer. I would not be at all surprised to hear that the enslaved people of Jamaica have risen up again and taken control of the island."

One year after Samuel Sharpe's death, slavery was abolished in the British colonies. However, these freed slaves were still expected to work for their previous owners as apprentices. Eventually on 1st August 1838, the Assembly in Jamaica ended this system of apprenticeships and declared total freedom.

In the re-built chapels of Jamaica, services were held as people waited for the start of their first day of freedom. In William Knibb's church a clock began to strike twelve as midnight approached. On the last strike of the clock, Knibb shouted, "The monster is dead; freedom has come!"

The sacrifices of Sam Sharpe and the other people who died in the slave rebellion of Christmas 1831 were not forgotten. Sharpe was reburied with honour in his chapel in Montego Bay. Then when Jamaica became an independent country in 1975, Samuel Sharpe was declared a National Hero.

At a Glance: Sam Sharpe

Sam Sharpe was born into slavery on Jamaica in 1801. He was educated and became a deacon at the Burchell Baptist Church in Montego Bay. By reading newspapers, Sharpe learnt about the abolition movement in Britain so he organised a general strike to demand that all slaves should be paid for their work. However, the rebellion quickly led to violence with the burning of sugar plantations and property. Sam Sharpe was captured and executed in 1832.

As a result of this uprising, missionaries from Jamaica went to Britain to campaign for the end of slavery, which happened in 1833. One week after the death of Sam Sharpe, the British government set up a committee to plan for the end of slavery. Today Sam Sharpe is one of Jamaica's National Heroes.

Fact file: The British Slavery Abolition Act

1 The abolition campaign became one of the largest mass movements in 19th century Britain. Eventually the British Government passed the Slavery Abolition Act on 24 August 1833. This gave freedom to all slaves in the British Empire.

2 The government agreed to pay a total of £20 million in compensation to slave-owners. There was no compensation for ex-slaves.

3 The Act did not lead to immediate freedom for slaves, as it did not become law until August 1st 1834. The law also allowed for a period when slaves had to work as "apprentices". People over six years old were expected to work for their masters for up to six years, with no pay except food, shelter and clothing.

5 However, it was impossible to make free people continue to work in this way and so four years later the apprenticeship system was abolished. On August 1st 1838, full freedom was given to the enslaved people of the British Empire.

6 Today, former British colonies in the Caribbean remember this event every August. This is known as Emancipation Day.

Faith in action

Sam Sharpe was a preacher. At a time when enslaved people were generally not taught to read and write, Sharpe was able to read the Bible for himself. He shared this knowledge with people working in plantations near his home.

We do not know what Sharpe preached. However, we do know that he believed that the Bible taught that no person should be enslaved. The following verses would have helped Sharpe to come to this understanding: 'You are all sons of God through faith in Christ Jesus, for all of you who were baptized into Christ have clothed yourself with Christ. There is neither Jew nor Greek, slave nor free, male nor female, for you are all one in Christ Jesus.' Galatians 3:26-28

Talk About It

Find other Bible verses or teachings that would have encouraged Sam Sharpe. Look at the Faith behind the action sections in other chapters for some help. Why do you think that the Bible verses above continue to be very important for Christians today?

Make your voice heard

The abolition movement in Britain and in the United States of America used petitions as one way of fighting for the end of slavery. A petition is a document that makes a request or a complaint. Petitions are used to draw the government's attention to something that concerns the general public.

In 1788, 103 petitions were sent to the British Parliament with at least 60,000 signatures. After the slave uprising in Jamaica, the number of petitions grew. In 1833, 5020 petitions were presented to the British Government. 1,309,913 people had signed these petitions. Today petitions are still an important part of changing government policy. Many organisations campaigning for the end to modern slavery use petitions that can be signed on the Internet.

Have you every signed a petition? What was it for? You can make your voice heard in this way. Signing a petition shows people in power that we care about what is happening in our world today.

Harriet Tubman

 IN THE YEAR 1834, ENSLAVED PEOPLE LIVING IN countries that were governed by Britain were finally freed. However, in other countries slavery continued. In the United States of America, the country was divided. Some states, known as "free states", made slavery illegal, whilst other states continued to allow slavery.

Many people living as slaves sought freedom for themselves and ran away from their owners. Their aim was to reach areas of America where they could live as free people. However in 1850, a new law, called the Fugitive Slave Law, was introduced in the United States. This allowed slave owners to re-capture their runaway slaves from "free states".

As a result, people escaping from slavery, now had to travel to Canada if they wanted to be free from capture. At that time Canada was governed by Britain. Slavery was illegal here and no one could be sent back to his or her owner, once they had crossed the Canadian border.

Running away was difficult and dangerous. People who were against slavery tried to help enslaved people escaping from their owners.

They provided food, a safe place to spend the night and money. This became known as "The Underground Railroad". Those who guided people to safety were known as "conductors". Those who were fleeing from slavery were known as "passengers". People who helped runaway slaves had to work secretly and were always in danger of being arrested, imprisoned and fined. One of the women who became "a conductor" on this "Underground Railroad" was born in Maryland, in about 1822. Her name was Araminta Ross or Minty for short. Later in life she became known as Harriet Tubman.

Minty had escaped. She had run as fast as possible out of the house and away from her angry mistress, Miss Susan. Past the neighbour's houses, past the slave cabins, past the fields of corn she ran, not daring to look back or to stop to catch her breath. Finally the shouts of her mistress and master faded in the distance.

Crossing a field, the seven-year-old girl saw a pigsty. Grabbing the wooden fence, she pulled herself over the top and tumbled into the pen. A large sow lifted her head to see what was going on and grunted at being disturbed.

Minty huddled at the back of the pigsty, trying to make her body as small as possible. "I won't go back! I won't go back!" she cried to herself.

Minty belonged to Edward Brodess. However, from the age of 6, he had hired her out to work for other people. Miss Susan had taken Minty to work in her house and to help look after her young baby. Right from the start, Minty found herself in trouble.

"Clean this room!" Miss Susan instructed her. Minty tried her best. She swept the room and immediately wiped the table and chairs with a cloth. However the dust from the sweeping was still in the air and soon fell back upon the furniture. When Miss Susan came to see how Minty was doing, she was furious.

"There's dust everywhere!" she shouted at the frightened girl.

Yet however hard Minty tried she could not get rid of the dust in the room. Finally Miss Susan went for her whip and began to hit Minty. Minty cried out in pain.

"What are you doing?" Miss Susan's sister, Emily, had come into the room. "Why are you whipping the poor girl?"

"Can't you see? This girl is lazy. I asked her to clean this room but look at it. It's filthy!" Miss Susan lowered the whip

Miss Emily smiled kindly at Minty. "You can't whip the child for not doing the cleaning properly. She has never been taught how to do it. Leave her with me." With careful teaching, Minty soon learnt how to clean the room. Yet there were other tasks that would prove even more difficult.

After a hard day's work, Minty had to look after Miss Susan's baby during the night. It was her duty to sleep next to the cot and to keep the baby from crying out. For hour after hour, Minty tried to keep awake and to rock the cradle.

However, it was impossible for Minty to keep awake through the whole night. Whenever the baby cried loud enough to wake Miss Susan, Minty was punished with the whip. Constantly tired and afraid of being whipped, Minty longed for her home and the love of her mother.

Miss Susan was the sort of person who became angry easily. This included being angry with her husband. One Friday morning, Miss Susan was shouting at him. Minty stood nervously nearby next to the kitchen table.

Suddenly Minty realised that no one was watching her and on the table stood a bowl of sugar lumps. Minty was never allowed to have sugar or to eat any sweet cakes or biscuits. Surely no one will notice if I take just one sugar lump, she thought to herself.

Quietly she moved towards the table and slowly reached out her fingers. Just as she was about to take one of the tempting sugar lumps, Miss Susan suddenly turned around.

"You thief!" she screamed and immediately reached to get her whip. Minty could take no more. Before Miss Susan's husband could block the door, Minty was gone. Without a thought or a plan, the little girl had made her dash for freedom.

However, now as the light was beginning to fade and the stars were appearing one by one, Minty did not know what to do. Where could she run? Who could she go to for help?

For the next three days, Minty stayed hidden in the pigsty. When the food for the pigs was thrown into the trough, she would wait until the farm worker had gone away and then she would try and grab as much of the food as possible. But the old mother pig did not like this stranger taking the food from her piglets. By Tuesday morning, Minty could stay there no longer.

Hungry, tired and miserable, Minty had no choice. Knowing that she would be punished, she walked slowly back to her master's house. When the master returned home at the end of the day, Minty's punishment began.

He beat her so hard that Minty could not move with the pain. Miss Susan sent her back to her owner, Mr. Brodess, with the words, "She's not worth a sixpence."

Twenty years later, Minty would run away again. However this time she would not return.

In 1849, Minty lay seriously ill. She was now married to a free man, John Tubman. Yet life had continued to be hard for her. As a young teenager, she had been hit on the head by a large piece of metal. This had broken her skull and left her with a brain injury which caused her pain and gave her black outs. Years of hard labour had also made her unwell. As she lay, tossing with a fever, the door of the cabin opened.

"There she is, the slave I want to sell. She may be ill now, but when she's working she's as strong as any man!" Minty recognised the voice of her owner, Mr. Brodess.

"I don't believe it, just look at her! She's not going to last long, if you ask me," another man grunted.

"But I'm offering her at the lowest price. Surely, you can't resist a bargain?"

The two men left Minty's cabin still discussing her price. In the gloom of the cabin, Minty tried to hold back the tears.

"Oh dear Lord, don't let him sell me. Don't let him take me away from John and my family," she pleaded with God.

Minty prayed constantly for her owner, begging God to save him. "Change his heart," she would cry, "Make him a Christian." But Brodess did not change his ways.

"Minty, listen to me," one of the girls who worked in Brodess's home whispered. "I heard the master talking last week at dinner. He said that as soon as you were better, he would sell you down South. And he is thinking of selling a couple of your brothers as well."

Minty understood what it meant to be sold South. She had seen two of her sisters taken away in a chain-gang to work in the cotton fields in the States further south. They were never heard of again. It had broken her parents' hearts. Now her prayer began to change.

"Lord, if you're not going to change that man's heart, then let him die. Take him out of the way, so that he can't do any more harm."

To Minty's horror, within a very short time that is exactly what happened. Edward Brodess died. Minty felt terrible that she had prayed for his death. She would have done anything to bring him back.

Furthermore, Brodess's death did not solve Minty's problems. No one knew what would happen now to the slaves that he had owned. Deep inside, Minty felt uneasy and thoughts of escape were constantly with her.

At night she had nightmares. Men on horseback were attacking a group of women and children. The screams of children being taken from their mothers would wake her up. Minty knew that the time had come to run away again. In her heart she kept hearing the words, "Arise, flee for your life!"

This time, Minty was prepared and knew where to go and what to do. Travelling at night, Minty followed the North Star to lead her in the right direction. Sometimes she slept in the open; sometimes people on the "Underground Railroad" gave her a place to sleep. Finally she reached the border and crossed into the "free state" of Pennsylvania.

As she walked across the border, Minty looked down at her hands to see if she was the same person. The sun broke through the clouds and covered the trees and fields with golden light. Minty felt as if she was in heaven. "I am free!" she cried.

But then she remembered her family back home and realised that now she was all alone. "If God will help me, I will make a home here and bring my family to join me. If I am free, my family should be free as well," she vowed. Then she asked God for help.

"Oh dear Lord, you are the only friend I have. Come to my help. I'm going to hold steady on to you and I know you'll see me through".

Minty started her new life by changing her name to Harriet. She had also decided to use her freedom to free others, and so she began to plan just how to do it.

It was not long before Tubman took action. The news came to her that her niece, Kessiah, with her two children, was about to be sold in a public auction. Tubman hurried down to Baltimore where she met up with Kessiah's husband, John Bowley. With little time to spare the two planned what to do.

On the day of the auction, Kessiah and her young children were brought to the front of the courthouse doors. A crowd of people had already gathered. When the auction began, buyers began to shout out the price they wanted to pay. Kessiah stood with her head bowed and her arms around her children, as the amount for her purchase rose. Finally John Brodess nodded. He was happy with the price and the auctioneer stopped the sale.

It was now well past lunch time, and the auctioneer was hungry. The sale of Kessiah was interrupted as he went off to eat. Kessiah would have to wait for his return.

Finally the auctioneer had finished his lunch break. "Will the buyer please step forward and make his payment?" he called out to the crowd in front of the courthouse. No one moved.

"Who has bought this slave and her children?" the auctioneer called again.

Someone shouted from the back of the crowd. "It was John Bowley. The husband of the slave."

John Bowley was nowhere to be seen. Annoyed at having wasted so much time, the auctioneer started the bidding again. However, the crowd was whispering. Nobody seemed to want to place a bid. When the auctioneer looked around, he realised why.

Kessiah and her children were no longer there; they had disappeared. With great embarrassment, the auctioneer stopped the bidding. How would he explain this to John Brodess?

Unknown to the auctioneer, when he had gone for lunch, John Bowley had simply walked away with his wife and children. He had taken them to a safe house not far away, where they waited in fear that at any moment they might be discovered. Later that day, the family made their way to the river and escaped in a canoe along the river to Baltimore.

Tubman was waiting for them and greeted them with relief. She hid Kessiah and her children until it was safe enough to take them across the state border to freedom.

This was just the first of nineteen such trips that Tubman made to help her family and other people escape from slavery. There was immense danger in working on the "Underground Railroad". The greatest danger for Tubman was that she would be captured and returned to the Brodess family.

However, she trusted God for her safety. Before making any trip, Tubman used to pray and would only make the journey if she felt that God was telling her to do so. In any moment of danger or difficulty, she would turn to God praying, "I'm going to hold steady onto you, and you've got to see me through."

Tubman was also very careful not to take unnecessary risks. She knew that the path to freedom was hard and difficult. It was easy for people to give up hope in the dark and cold and want to return to the plantations where they had lived. Tubman knew that if this happened, it would not be long before everyone would be in danger of being captured. Furthermore the identity of the people who helped her on the "Underground Railroad" could also be discovered.

To stop this happening, Tubman carried a gun. When someone gave up the courage or strength to carry on she would threaten him or her with the gun, "You can't give up now. You will go on or you will die!" Tubman never had to use her gun; she always managed to persuade her exhausted passengers to carry on.

One of the most dangerous trips that Tubman made was when she helped Joe Bailey and his brother, Bill, to escape.

Joe Bailey was a very valuable slave. His owner hired him out for a good sum of money to work on Hughlett's farm and timber plantation. For six years, Joe worked hard for his master. He became the foreman and Joe was such a good worker that his master decided that he wanted to own him, rather than hiring him. Hughlett agreed to pay two thousand dollars to Joe's owner. The morning after Hughlett had purchased Bailey, he rode up to Joe's cabin and called his name.

"You belong to me now," he informed Bailey. "Take off your shirt." Bailey did not know what to say.

"Take off your shirt, I say," Hughlett shouted. "It is my custom to whip every new slave that I have."

"But I have worked faithfully for you for the last six years. In that time, have I done anything wrong? There is no need to whip me."

But Hughlett would not listen to Bailey's pleas.

After the flogging, Bailey lay in his cabin with his back torn and bleeding. In the darkness, Bailey made a vow, "I will never again be whipped". From that moment he began to plan his escape.

Bailey knew about Tubman and her visits to the area to free her family. Whenever the enslaved plantation workers talked about her, they always called her "Moses", because Moses in the Bible took the people of Israel from slavery to the promised land of freedom. As soon as he could, he went to visit Tubman's father, Ben Ross.

"Ben, next time Moses comes this way, tell her that I am ready to go."

It was mid-November when Harriet Tubman returned. Joe Bailey, Bill Baley, Peter Pennington and Eliza Manokey set out to make their escape. Right from the start the journey was to prove dangerous. Hughlett found out that Joe had escaped almost immediately. He sent out the dogs to try and track him down. He hired slave catchers and printed posters offering a reward of $1,500 for Joe's capture. Joe Bailey was so valuable to Hughlett that no expense would be spared to track him down. Both Bill and Peter's owners also offered rewards for their capture.

Tubman did everything she could to keep her passengers safe. They went round in circles, wore disguises and stayed hidden in safe houses for longer than Tubman would have liked. Eventually they reached Wilmington, but Hughlett and the other owners had already arrived. They had put posters everywhere and a check point had been set up on the bridge crossing the river.

Tubman knew that it was impossible for them to cross without being captured so she sent word to Thomas Garrett who worked on the "Underground Railroad" and who was going to help them make the next stage of their journey.

Garrett lost no time. He arranged for two wagons carrying bricks to be sent across the river. In the wagons were secret compartments. The bricklayers hid the escaping people in the wagons and at the end of the day drove it back across the river whilst the slave catchers and police waved them on.

Eventually the group reached New York. Yet even here, Joe Bailey was not safe from re-capture. Posters were everywhere and people were easily able to identify the tall, strong man.

"How far is it to Canada?" Bailey asked

Joe was shown a map of New York State. On it was marked the railway line that would take them to the border at Niagara Falls. There were over 300 miles still to travel.

Bailey sat down with his head in his hands. With posters offering so much money for his capture, surely someone would hand him over to the authorities. "I will never escape" he murmured in despair.

"Don't give up now Joe," Tubman tried to encourage him. "The Lord has been with us so far, he will not leave us now."

Despite the added danger of helping Bailey, Tubman continued the journey to Canada. Bailey was now totally silent as he travelled on the train. He just sat with his head in his hands. All he could think about was what would happen to him if he were re-captured.

At last, the tired group reached the bridge that would take them into Canada. In excitement everyone was looking at the beautiful waterfalls. Joe still remained silent and did not dare look out at the sight. In the middle of the bridge, once they had crossed the border, Tubman went to sit by him. "You are free now," Tubman gently shook him. "No one can take you back now."

Finally Joe Bailing broke his silence. In total relief he began to sing as loudly as he could, giving thanks to God,

"Glory to God and Jesus too,
One more soul got safe;
Oh, go and carry the news,
One more soul got safe."

Once he stepped off the train, Bailey continued to sing. He made so much noise that soon a group of men and women had surrounded him. One of the finely dressed ladies, handed him a handkerchief so that he could wipe the tears from his eyes.

"Thank the Lord!" Joe declared.

"There's only one more journey for me now, and that's to heaven."

In her old age, when Tubman looked back over her life, she was able to say, "On my underground railroad I never ran my train off the track and I never lost a passenger."

Tubman helped about 300 people to escape from slavery. She was one of the few "conductors" never to be caught or to lose someone that she was helping to escape. She also encouraged and gave instructions to help many more people run away by themselves.

When asked about her courage and her escapes from danger, she used to say, "I tell you, it wasn't me. It was the Lord. As long as Jesus wanted to use me, he would take care of me. And when he didn't want me any longer, I was ready to go."

As well as helping people to escape from slavery, Tubman also worked with people who were trying to end slavery in the United States. It was whilst she was staying with one of these abolitionists, the Rev. Garnet, that Tubman had a dream in the night.

Rev. Garnet could hear his guest singing as she came down the stairs for breakfast the next morning. Her words were clear, "My people are free! My people are free!"

"Now, Harriet do stop singing and come and have something to eat," Rev. Garnet said to his excited visitor. But Tubman could not eat. All she could think about was the dream that had come to her in the night. In her dream she saw the end of slavery in America.

"Harriet, you are tormenting us!" Mr. Garnet pleaded.

"My grandchildren may see the day when all slaves will be free, but it will certainly not happen when you and I are alive."

Tubman shook her head in disagreement.

"I tell you, sir, you will see that day. And you will see it soon. My people are free!"

Harriet Tubman was right. Three years later President Lincoln published a document called "The Emancipation Proclamation." On the first of January 1863, everyone held as a slave within the United States was pronounced free. Slavery had been banned in America.

At a Glance: Harriet Tubman

In 1849, Harriet Tubman escaped from slavery in the American state of Maryland. The next year she became a conductor for the Underground Railroad and helped other slaves to escape to freedom. Over the next ten years she made about nineteen rescue trips and rescued over 300 people. Many of these people were her friends and members of her family. She helped more people escape by giving them practical advice and encouragement.

Tubman supported the abolition movement and its leaders. She was a favourite speaker at antislavery meetings. During the American Civil War, Tubman worked as a nurse, scout and spy for the Union. During this time she helped to liberate slaves during military raids on southern plantations.

After the war, she lived in Auburn, New York, and was an active member of the American Methodist Episcopal Zion Church. She worked for the voting rights of black people and founded the Harriet Tubman Home for Aged Negroes. Harriet Tubman died in 1913.

Fact file: The Underground Railroad

1. The Underground Railroad was the name given to the large network of people in America who helped fugitive slaves escape to northern free states, to Canada and even to British colonies in the West Indies.

2. People who opposed slavery gave shelter, food and money to escaping slaves. The homes that were used to hide fugitives were called "stations".

3. Some people were also known as "conductors". A conductor was someone who helped guide people to safety.

4. It is difficult to know how many people escaped slavery this way because it was dangerous for people working on the Underground Railroad to keep records. However some people estimate that 50,000 people had escaped from the South by 1850. Other estimates suggest as many as 100,000 slaves escaped.

5. However, by 1850 plantation owners were so worried about the number of slaves escaping that they managed to persuade the American government to pass the Fugitive Slave Act. This act meant that anyone in America who helped a runaway slave would be fined and even sent to prison.

6 The Fugative Slave Act failed to stop the Underground Railroad, due to the bravery of those who were escaping and the bravery of those who were prepared to face fines, prison and even death for helping people gain their freedom.

Faith in action

Harriet Tubman trusted God and talked to him about her needs. When facing danger she used to pray: 'Oh Lord! You've been with me through six troubles, don't desert me in the seventh!' She believed that her life was totally in God's hands, and that He would take care of her until it was time for her to die. God had helped her in the past, was able to help in the present and would continue to be with her in the future. Today Harriet Tubman is famous for her bravery and courage. When we believe that God is in control of our lives, we need not be afraid to do what is right. We can trust God to give us strength and to meet our needs.

Talk about it

Harriet Tubman used the code name "Moses". Moses was an important person in the Old Testament. He led the people of Israel out of slavery in Egypt. Find out more about the story by reading Exodus Chapters 1 - 15. You could also watch the film, The Prince of Egypt, by Dreamworks Pictures. Why was the story of Moses important to Harriet Tubman and other enslaved people? How did this Bible story give people hope?

Make Your Voice Heard

Visit websites for groups such as Christian Solidarity Worldwide and Open Doors who support persecuted peoples around the world. Christian Solidarity Worldwide can help you to keep in touch with people in other countries who need help and encouragement. They can also give you advice about how to write a letter to your M.P. when you are concerned about a specific issue.

Pray to God about your life and trust him with it. Ask Him for the courage to be brave and to stand up for truth and justice, not just in big campaigns but in your daily life. Ask God to give you the strength to fight for the rights of others.

Harriet Beecher Stowe

 NOT FAR FROM HARRIET TUBMAN'S HOME IN Maryland, a black minister, the Rev. Samuel Green, was reading a book. The curtains were pulled tightly across the window, as the minister read to his wife in a quiet voice. The book they were reading was called *Uncle Tom's Cabin*. The story of *Uncle Tom's Cabin* begins with a slave owner, Mr. Shelby, doing business with a slave trader, Haley. The deal is done. Uncle Tom and a four year old boy, called Harry, were to be sold to pay off some of Mr. Shelby's debts.

However, Harry's mother, Eliza, overhears the conversation. Immediately she prepares to run away with her child. She warns Uncle Tom that the next day, he too, will be separated from his wife and family. Yet Uncle Tom decides not to run away because if he ran away other enslaved people would have to be sold in his place.

Eliza manages to escape with the help of people on the "Underground Railroad". Eventually her husband joins her in Canada where they can live in freedom. However, Uncle Tom is never reunited with his family. Sold to various owners, he is finally owned by a violent and cruel man, Legree. When two of Legree's slaves run away, Tom refuses to tell his master where they have gone. Legree beats Tom so badly that he never recovers. Trusting in God's love and forgiving his master for his cruelty, Tom dies. The Rev. Green closed the book with a sigh.

"How can people say that this book is untrue?" asked his wife, Catherine. "I've even heard people saying that slaves are treated well and are quite happy to work for nothing. What nonsense!"

The Rev. Green smiled at his wife. He knew that she was right. In his mind he began to list the names of people he knew, who just like Eliza in the book, had run away in order to try and save their families from being sold to a new owner or from being separated.

Even his own son, Sam, had fled to Canada and everyday he had waited prayerfully, hoping for news of his safety. Finally a letter had arrived. His son was safe and well with plenty of friends and plenty of food. The Rev. Green had carefully folded the letter and hidden it out of sight.

The Rev. Green also knew all about the "Underground Railroad", because he was part of it and had helped many escape to freedom. In fact he had helped Joe Bailey when he was escaping with Harriet Tubman. The minister knew that it was illegal in Maryland to help runaway slaves and he also knew that it was illegal in Maryland to own a book that called for the abolition of slavery. Being part of the "Underground Railroad" meant that he and his wife had to be constantly on alert. They also had to be very careful about what they said and did in public.

It was, however, impossible to keep everything secret. The authorities began to watch the Rev. Green. By 1857, the local plantation owners were certain that the minister was part of the "Underground Railroad". Something had to be done to stop him.

"Open up!" Someone banged on the door.

"It's Sheriff Bell and I've got a search warrant."

The Rev. Green looked at Catherine, and tried to speak.

"My dear," Catherine reached out her hand to her husband. There was nothing to say. They had always known that the day could come when they would be arrested for being part of the "Underground Railway". Quietly she began to pray as her husband pulled back the bolt on the door. The Sheriff and his men began to search the house and the sheds outside.

"So where do you keep these runaways?" the Sheriff asked finally as his men reported back that they had found no one. The Rev. Green said nothing.

"And what about this?" the Sheriff continued as he threw a pile of papers and books down on the table. The Rev. Green glanced down at the documents. There were the letters from his son, maps and railroad timetables. On top of the letters was his book, Uncle Tom's Cabin.

"You're under arrest!" the Sheriff finally announced. "I am arresting you for helping slaves to escape and for owning material that could cause people of colour to be discontent and to rebel."

There was not enough evidence to prove that the Rev. Samuel Green was part of the "Underground Railroad". However, the court still jailed him. His copy of *Uncle Tom's Cabin* was considered enough to show that he was guilty of stirring up trouble amongst the enslaved people in his neighbourhood. Five years later, in 1862, he was released from prison and ordered to leave the State of Maryland.

The Rev. Green had lost his freedom and his home because of a book; a book that was written by a woman who lived in a free state and had only visited the slave owning South once in her life. This woman was called Harriet Beecher Stowe and this is the story of how she came to write one of the most important novels ever written by an American. The story began just as Stowe was moving from Cincinnati to live in Brunswick.

Tired from the journey and having to look after her six children, Harriet Beecher Stowe arrived at her brother's home in Boston. She was planning to spend a few days before moving on to her new home. Whilst Stowe's thoughts were troubled with all she had to do, her brother and sister-in-law were concerned with what was happening in the country.

A new law was about to be approved, called the Fugitive Slave Law. This law would give the slave owners of the South, the right to enter the free states and to re-capture any person who had escaped from slavery. The law would also make it illegal to help people escaping from slavery.

"It's a shameful, wicked, abominable law!" her sister-in-law Isabella cried. Harriet's brother Edward nodded his head in agreement. Harriet was troubled at the conversation.

"Whenever I think about the subject of slavery, I have an over whelming desire to do something about it. But what can I do?" she admitted to her family.

One person had a very clear idea of what Harriet could do about the Fugitive Slave Law. After Harriet had left for her new home, Isabella continued the discussion by writing letters describing what was happening in Boston as a result of the new law. At the end of one of these letters, Isabella wrote some words that were to help Harriet Stowe finally make up her mind.

When she received this letter she opened it up and began to read it to the whole family. "Now Hattie, if I could use my pen as you can, I would write something that would make this whole nation feel what a terrible thing slavery is."

Everyone was quiet in the room. Slowly Stowe rose from her chair, crushing the letter in her hand. "I will write something. I will, as long as I live."

Yet still Harriet hesitated. Her mind was full of doubts. First, Stowe would need a good story, a story that would interest her readers. She would also need to know what she was writing about. The subject of slavery was a difficult one. She knew something about it from her own experiences and from what she had heard and read. But was that enough to write a book?

On top of this, Harriet Stowe faced the constant problem of trying to be a mother and a writer at the same time. How could she find the time to write a book on such a difficult subject? Her baby kept her awake at night, and left her feeling exhausted. Wherever she went in the house, there were children playing and demanding her attention. How would she ever get the peace and quiet she needed for serious writing?

Her family continued to encourage her. This time it was her brother, Henry Ward, who decided to talk to her.

Arriving on a dark, cold January night, Henry sat with his sister as the wind howled around the house. "We have to show people who go to church, how evil slavery is," he stressed.

Harriet told her brother about Isabella's letter. "I will do my part to fight the Fugitive Slave Law," she reassured him.

"That's wonderful news, Harriet. You finish your story and I will help to make sure that people read it."

Shortly after that visit from her brother, Harriet Stowe had an experience that would help her finally take up her pen and begin to write. One Sunday in February, she was at church. It was a communion service. As she prayed and remembered the death of Jesus, a picture suddenly began to form in her mind.

In her mind she saw an old black man, being beaten with whips. A white plantation owner was standing nearby watching the punishment. She heard the old man cry to God to have mercy on his torturers. The vision filled her thoughts and for a moment she was no longer aware of what was happening in the church.

By the end of the church service, Harriet knew that this was what she had needed. This was the story that she had to tell; the story of a Christian man whose freedom and whose life had been taken from him. She would call him Tom. Rushing home from church, Stowe grabbed her notepad and began to write.

Later that day she read what she had written to her children. They were deeply moved at the story. By the end Henry, one of her sons, exclaimed, "Oh mama! Slavery is the most cruel thing in the world."

Yet still Harriet Stowe had doubts. Did she know enough about slavery to bring her story to life? Did she have enough facts to make it accurate?

For a moment, Harriet Stowe stopped writing and closed her eyes. In her mind she was back in Cincinnati, in the state of Ohio. Kentucky, a slave state, lay just across the Ohio River. Within Cincinnati there was a community of African Americans. Some of these people were freed slaves. Some had run away from Kentucky. Others had bought or been given their freedom. Harriet thought back to the day when a thin, and poorly dressed black girl came and knocked at her door.

"Please can you give me a job?" the girl asked. "My mistress has left me here and gone back to Kentucky. I have no way of providing for myself."

Harriet stood with her youngest baby in her arms.

"What's your name?"

"Mina," came the reply.

The scream of another child came from the kitchen. I certainly could do with some help with the housework, Harriet thought to herself. Her need to find time to write was worrying her. She had promised a story to a magazine and yet it seemed impossible to get it finished by the date she had promised. However, there was little money to pay for a servant.

"Mina, you can stay with us. But I cannot pay you a very good wage," she admitted. Mina was happy to accept the offer of a home.

As the two women worked together in the house they began to learn about each other's lives. Harriet tried to teach Mina about the Bible and about Jesus Christ. She soon realised that she would have to start right from the beginning when Mina admitted that she did not even know who Jesus Christ was. Harriet could not believe that this was possible.

"Haven't you ever seen a Bible?" she asked.

"Yes," Mina admitted.

"Sometimes I saw my mistress reading the Bible. But I don't think it did her any good!" As Harriet taught Mina how to look after the house, Mina talked about her home and life in Kentucky.

"I was scared of my mistress," Mina admitted. " She used to beat me for the slightest mistake."

One evening, Harriet turned to her husband, "Calvin, I'm worried about Mina. What will happen if her mistress returns?" Professor Stowe was not sure but promised to find out. Within the week, he reported back to his wife.

"Well, my dear, Mina will be pleased to hear that according to the laws of Ohio, she is in fact a free person. Her owner has left her and therefore she can no longer be considered a slave."

When Harriet shared the good news with Mina, she was strangely quiet. "What's the matter? I thought you would be pleased!"

"But Missus, no one will believe me when I say that I am free."

"Well then, we will have to take you to the magistrate. He will be able to give you papers showing that you are a free person."

Some time later Professor Stowe came home from work looking worried. "Harriet, I had better warn you. Today I heard that Mina's owner has arrived in Cincinnati. He is looking for her and wants to take her back to Kentucky."

"But how can that happen? She has her legal papers."

"Don't worry. I'll find out what we can do."

As soon as he could, Professor Stowe went back to the magistrate and explained the danger that Mina was now in.

"Surely, she cannot be sent back to Kentucky. Her papers are in order."

The magistrate peered over the top of his glasses. "Professor Stowe, that may be the case. But be warned, there is a judge here who is prepared to help slave owners. Mina's owner will come in the night with a warrant and an officer of the law. They will take her to this judge and he will hand Mina over to her master."

"But surely, that's illegal. There must be something that we could do?"

The magistrate shook his head.

"No, there will be nothing you can do to stop Mina being taken back into slavery. That will be the end."

"So what can we do?"

The magistrate lowered his voice and coughed. "Professor Stowe, between you and me, there is only one thing you can do at this time. Take her away from here, to a place of safety, where she can hide until the search for her comes to an end."

From time to time, the Stowe family were called upon to be part of the "Underground Railroad". They also knew other people in the area who helped runaway slaves. One of these people was John Van Zandt.

At one time Van Zandt had lived in Kentucky and had owned a number of people. Yet the time came when he no longer felt it was right to own another human being. He moved to the free state of Ohio and set all his slaves free. Now he was living in a forest, about ten miles away from the Stowes. His house was difficult to get to. It was only possible to reach it by crossing a fast-flowing creek.

That evening, the Stowe family and Mina waited nervously until it was dark. Then when the time had come, Harriet's brother and the Professor took their guns, and helped Mina up into a covered wagon.

"Do be careful of the creek," Harriet whispered as her husband took the reigns of the horses. By the time they arrived at Van Zandt's house, it was midnight. Professor Stowe knocked on the door. The owner of the house came to the door. By the light of a flickering candle, Van Zandt peered out.

"Are you a man, who would help a poor black girl from being kidnapped?

"Guess I am!" came the reply. "But how did you get here?"

"We crossed the creek."

"Well, the Lord must have helped you," Van Zandt exclaimed. "I wouldn't dare to cross that creek in the night. A man and his family were drowned there, only a little while ago." He then turned to Mina who was hiding in the shadows.

"Come in side, my dear. You will be safe with us."

Harriet opened her eyes and smiled as she remembered Mina. John Van Zandt kept Mina hidden and so she was never captured. Instead she got married and had a large family of children. Harriet began to make notes about Mina's escape. "That's one story I can use in my book," she thought. She also wrote letters to her husband who was continuing to work in Cincinnati for a little longer, asking for information. "Can you find out how much Willie Watson paid to buy his friend's freedom?" she asked.

To another friend she wrote, "Some of my story is going to take place in a cotton plantation. I have some information about these plantations, but I really need to know more. I want my writing to be as accurate as possible." So piece by piece, Harriet collected the information she needed.

"I have to know that my work will be published. I cannot spend the time writing a book if no one will be able to read it," she explained to her husband. Eventually a newspaper called the National Era agreed to publish her story in monthly parts. The editor also agreed to pay Stowe for her work, so now she could relax and really get to work.

As for finding the time to write, Stowe turned to her sister, Catherine, for help. Catherine came to live with the Stowe family and by this time Harriet's husband had also moved from Cincinnati. Breakfast and family prayers were finished by 8 o'clock. Then Catherine would take over the running of the home, whilst Harriet went with her husband to write in his office in the college where he worked. Getting out of the house was the only way that the book would be written. There was just too much going on. So finally, despite all the problems, Stowe picked up her pen to write the last pages of *Uncle Tom's Cabin*. "Everyone can do something to fight the wickedness of slavery," she concluded.

Uncle Tom's Cabin was published as a book in March 1852. Harriet Beecher Stowe was amazed at the response. On the very first day, the book sold three thousand copies. By the end of the year it had sold three hundred thousand copies in America.

The story of Uncle Tom moved people to take action against slavery. As a result of the book, many people refused to obey the Fugitive Slave Act and continued to help people escaping from the South. Many more people began to call for the abolition of slavery.

As a teenager, Harriet had given her abilities and talents to God. She wrote to her brother these words, "It matters little what service He has for me. I do not mean to live in vain. He has given me talents, and I will lay them at his feet, well satisfied, if He will accept them."

Harriet Beecher Stowe was faithful to that commitment and used her writing abilities and talents to help bring an end to slavery in the United States of America.

At a Glance: Harriet Beecher Stowe

Harriet Beecher Stowe was the author of Uncle Tom's Cabin. It was originally published in 1951 as a serial story for the Washington anti-slavery newspaper, the National Era. Uncle Tom's Cabin was a story that described the physical and emotional abuse of enslaved people. It also showed the bravery, resistance to slavery and Christian faith of many enslaved African Americans. The book was an instant best seller, and made Beecher Stowe a celebrity. She was invited to Britain and other European countries to speak against slavery.

Harriet was heavily criticised for this book. Some people said that she had lied about the condition of enslaved people in the South. She wrote another book A Key to Uncle Tom's Cabin to show that her story was based on fact.

When Abraham Lincoln met Harriet Beecher Stowe in 1862 he said, "So you're the little woman who wrote the book that started this Great War!" Uncle Tom's Cabin inspired people to demand freedom for all Americans.

Fact file: Slavery in the United States

1. Enslaved black people first came to America in the early 17th century.

2. The abolition movement in American grew in strength during the 18th century. After the American Revolution (1775-1783) steps were taken to encourage the abolition of slavery: Northern states were to abolish slavery; A number of states passed acts to make it easier for slave owners to free their slaves

3. In 1808 the importation of enslaved Africans was made illegal. It is estimated that at least 300,000 people had been brought to the USA as slaves.

4. Most slaves worked on plantations to produce sugar, tobacco, coffee and cotton. They also worked as domestic workers, trades people and in industry.

5. Despite the end of the slave trade, slavery continued in the southern States. By 1860, there were about 4 million slaves in the USA. Slave holding states refused to abolish slavery.

6. In 1865, slavery in the USA was finally made illegal by the 13th Amendment of the Constitution.

7. Overcoming the negative effects of slavery led to the civil rights movement in the 20th century and the struggle for equal rights for black people.

Faith in action

The people who helped to bring about the abolition of slavery all had different backgrounds, abilities and jobs. Harriet was a mother who spent most of her time looking after her children. She was also a writer and wanted God to use her talents. Whatever we end up doing with our lives, we will also have opportunities to serve God and to make a difference in this world. If we give God our abilities, he will accept them and use our lives to help others.

Talk about it

Many of the leaders of the abolition movement were Christians. However, there were Christians who supported slavery. Some preachers and slave-owners used Bible verses to support their actions. However, they failed to look at the whole teaching of the Bible, which teaches that injustice and exploitation is wrong. Harriet considered that slavery was a sin against God. She called upon people to turn away from it. Sometimes we can think that we are doing the right thing, when in fact we are wrong. Sometimes we are not even aware that we are living in a way that displeases God. How do you think we can avoid this happening?

Make your voice heard

Harriet hoped that her book would help to change racist attitudes. She wrote to her young readers: *"…when you grow up, I hope the foolish and unchristian prejudice against people merely on account of their complexion will be done away with."* Sadly, this did not happen. Racism still exists. What can we do to help build a just society? Here are a few ideas: Celebrate your own culture and the culture of others; Make friends with people from different races and cultures; Report racist bullying at school; Do not say jokes that insult other races, religions or cultures; Support anti-racist organisations and campaigns

Pray to God to show you what is in your heart and in your thoughts. Ask him to examine the way you live so that you can see what things in your life displease him. Ask God to speak to you through your conscience, so you will know when you are thinking, saying or doing wrong. Ask the LORD to guide you and to make your life one of love, truth and justice.

David Livingstone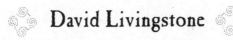

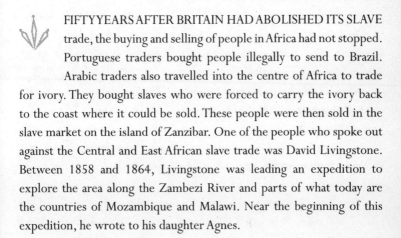

FIFTY YEARS AFTER BRITAIN HAD ABOLISHED ITS SLAVE trade, the buying and selling of people in Africa had not stopped. Portuguese traders bought people illegally to send to Brazil. Arabic traders also travelled into the centre of Africa to trade for ivory. They bought slaves who were forced to carry the ivory back to the coast where it could be sold. These people were then sold in the slave market on the island of Zanzibar. One of the people who spoke out against the Central and East African slave trade was David Livingstone. Between 1858 and 1864, Livingstone was leading an expedition to explore the area along the Zambezi River and parts of what today are the countries of Mozambique and Malawi. Near the beginning of this expedition, he wrote to his daughter Agnes.

Dear Agnes,
Near Lake Shirwa we met a group of slave-traders. We saw the sticks that they use to imprison people whom they have just bought. These sticks can be up to eight feet long. The neck is

put into a space at the end of the stick. After a while, this stick is removed and the slave is then put in chains.

I am working in the hope that in the course of time this vile system will end…

Chief Chibisa invited the Scottish explorer to sit with him. There was an important matter to discuss. Chief Chibisa's wife was in tears.

"A few years ago slave raiders came to our village. They stole our daughter," the chief explained. "We know she was taken to Tete and we have heard that she was sold to a Portuguese man. Please can you help us? We will pay any price to set her free again."

The next time that Livingstone passed through the town of Tete, he remembered his friend Chief Chibisa.

"I'm sorry Livingstone," the Portuguese man shrugged his shoulders. "If I had the girl, you could have her and return her to her parents. However, some time ago I sold her. I don't know where she went. Somewhere up north I think."

When Livingstone finally returned to Chibisa's village, he told the chief and his wife what he had found out. There was nothing further that Livingstone could say. They would never see their daughter again.

As Livingstone and his expedition crossed the country, they found themselves using well-established slave routes and following the roads used by Arab traders.

"Don't stay here out in the open," an old chief warned as he walked out of his village towards Livingstone's party. The chief was called Mosauka. He welcomed the tired travellers and gave them a goat and a basket of food. As the men ate, Mosauka chatted to his guests.

"You must sleep in my village tonight. There is a slave party camping nearby. They are on their way to the coast and are carrying a large number of people."

At that moment, six men wearing long robes and carrying guns, walked into the village. The men had come from the slave caravan.

"We have some young children for sale," they announced.

Mosauka quickly explained that the travellers were English and did not buy slaves. The traders looked at each other and left immediately. They knew that the English were trying to stop the slave trade. Returning to their camp, they moved everybody out under cover of darkness.

Later on Livingstone found out that some of the people who had been enslaved by this group of traders had in fact been rescued. They had reached the coast and been put on a boat. A British navel ship stopped the boat and released the prisoners.

The Makololo people, who travelled and worked with Livingstone, were disgusted by the slave traders that they met on their journeys.

"These men are yellow hearted. Why won't you let us choke them?"

However, Livingstone would not let the Makololo attack the traders, as he could not protect the slaves once they had been freed. Livingstone knew that fighting the slave traders would not stop the problem. The slave trade itself had to be stopped.

As well as slave traders, Livingstone also met chiefs who sold their own people into slavery. He listened to what they had to say and tried to understand why they did this.

"We do not sell many people," these chiefs tried to explain. "We only sell those who have committed crimes."

However, Livingstone also knew that in some cases this was not always true. People who were simply disliked by a chief could also be sold to the kidnappers. The financial rewards for selling people were sometimes too big a temptation. The price of a man was four yards of cotton cloth, three for a woman and two for a boy or girl. Livingstone realised that some of these chiefs only sold people into slavery because their communities were poor.

Therefore Livingstone thought that the best way to stop the selling of people was to develop the trade in cotton and sugar. If chiefs could buy goods through selling crops, that were easily grown in the rich soil around them, then there would no longer be any need to sell people to the slave traders.

However, the next time that Livingstone visited, the situation had only got worse. The Yao and the Ngoni peoples were raiding their neighbours. The whole country was at war, with large numbers of people being taken away as slaves to the coast. It was becoming increasingly dangerous for Livingstone and his companions to travel.

Yet the explorer had made a promise. He had agreed to take Bishop Mackenzie and a group of missionaries into the highlands of this region so that they could start a mission station.

One afternoon, Livingstone and his party stopped at the village where Mbame was the chief. "A slave party will be here soon," Mbame warned his visitors. Once again Livingstone and his travelling companions discussed what they should do.

"The situation is getting worse. Something has to be done."

"These enslaved people are our brothers. We must do something to help."

In this area, the people who were being taken as slaves were being sold to Portuguese merchants in Tete, who would then transport them across the Atlantic Ocean to Brazil. Livingstone was totally fed up with the fact that the Portuguese authorities seemed to do little to stop this illegal activity despite having made international agreements to do so.

"Yes, we must act. The Portuguese must learn that they cannot continue to trade in people," he agreed.

At that moment, the slave caravan began to enter the village. Livingstone was shocked at the sight of the captured people who looked as if they were on the verge of starvation. The majority of the people were boys and girls ranging from the ages of seven to fifteen years old. There were also many younger children amongst the group.

The young men amongst the group were forced to wear the slave sticks that previously Livingstone had described to his daughter, Agnes. The weight of these wooden sticks meant that every step they took was painful and difficult. The women were tied with rope made from the bark of trees. At first these were soft but as the bark dried they became as hard as iron, biting into their wrists and cutting their skin. The little children were tied to their mothers so that they could not run away.

Alongside this group of exhausted people marched the drivers. Some of them were blowing little tin trumpets to announce their arrival. All of them were carrying guns. These men were Africans, some of whom were slaves themselves. Livingstone immediately recognised the leader as someone who lived at Tete and who had been the slave of a Portuguese official there.

The slave drivers also recognised Livingstone and his colleagues. As soon as they saw the white men, these drivers ran as fast as they could and had soon vanished into the forest. However, one of the Makololo men had also acted quickly. He grabbed hold of the leader of the slave caravan and made him drop his gun.

"Where did you get these captives?" Livingstone asked.

"I bought them," came the reply.

However, Livingstone did not believe him. When they asked the captives how they had come to be taken as slaves, nearly all of them said that they had been captured in war.

Whilst this questioning was going on, the last of the slave raiders took his chance and managed to run from the village. Once the captives knew that all the slave raiders had disappeared they began to kneel down in the dust and clap with thankfulness. "We are free!" they cried.

As quickly as possible the 84 people were released. It was easy to cut the women and children free, but releasing the men with their wooden harnesses was much more of a problem. In the end, a saw was found in Bishop Mackenzie's luggage. Slowly, one by one, the men were cut free.

Once the women were freed they were told that they could take the food that they had been carrying on their heads and make breakfast. They took the slave sticks and used them to make a very large fire for cooking.

The released captives were now free to do whatever they wanted. However, all of them chose to stay with Livingstone's expedition and to go with the missionaries back into the highlands.

The next day, Livingstone and his companions continued their trek towards the hills. They walked along the paths that the slave caravan had travelled on. At one point Livingstone was shown the body of a dead man.

"This man was part of our group," he was told. "But he was unwell and could not keep up. One of the drivers killed him with an axe."

A little further on, Livingstone passed the body of a baby. The mother was so exhausted that she had not been able to carry the child. So again one of the slave-traders had killed the baby.

As well as witnessing the horrors of the slave caravans, Livingstone also saw the effects of the war that was leading to so many people being taken captives.

Crowds of refugees passed the expedition as they fled for safety. On their heads, they carried as much food as they could. In the deserted villages, the crops were ready to harvest. Now the corn and the pumpkins were being left to rot or be eaten by animals. Many of the villages had been destroyed by fire. The stores of corn had been wrecked and left scattered over the paths and fields. With the ruin of the harvest, these people would face famine in the coming months.

Eventually the time came for Livingstone to leave Bishop Mackenzie and the missionaries, in order to continue his expedition. Many of the freed captives decided to stay with the Bishop and help him set up a mission station.

One of the boys who had been released by Livingstone and his travelling companions was called Chuma.

"Let me come with you," the boy pleaded. Livingstone looked down at Chuma who had lost everything: his home, his family and almost his freedom.

"Yes, you can come with me," the explorer agreed. "But it will be hard work."

Chuma did not seem to mind and he was to become one of Livingstone's most experienced and committed travelling companions.

In 1864, the British government decided to end Livingstone's expedition. The doctor returned to Britain and wrote about what had happened. He described the slave trade in Africa and called for the Portuguese authorities to do more to stop the trade. People were now aware that the fight against slavery had not ended; there was still a long way to go.

Two years later, Livingstone returned to Africa. This time, his task was to explore central Africa in order to find the beginning of the great river Nile. He arrived on the island of Zanzibar, which was the centre of the Arab slave trade.

Livingstone watched the slave-dhows sailing in and out of the harbour. The island was under the control of the Sultan and the slave trade had made the Sultan and his merchants very rich.

One day Livingstone visited the slave market. There were about three hundred people waiting to be sold. Here their teeth were examined and their bodies prodded by possible buyers. Sometimes the slave trader would throw a stick and make one of his prisoners run after it, just to show that the person was fit and healthy. Other enslaved people were pulled around the market place by the hand, whilst their owner called out their price.

With relief, Livingstone finally left the island to start his journey in search of the River Nile. On this journey he would learn even more about the Arab merchants and the way they traded in people. Right from the start, Livingstone found that his travels would depend on these Arab traders. He used their paths and made his base in Ujiji, which was a trading town. Some of the Arab merchants became his friends and helped him when he was ill or in need of supplies.

Yet other traders caused Livingstone serious problems. One of the problems that Livingstone faced was getting his letters and reports back to the British authorities at the coast. The only way of sending letters was to give them to the Arab merchants who were travelling that way.

However, it was known that Livingstone was reporting about the slave trade and some of the merchants did not want Livingstone's reports to be read. Some people refused to carry his letters. Others agreed to take his post, but unfortunately "lost" the letters on the way.

Another reason why it became difficult to send letters back to the coast was that some African chiefs had began to attack the Arab merchants. These chiefs were determined to defend their people against the slave trade and wanted to stop the traders from travelling across or entering their lands. It became extremely dangerous for anyone to travel.

Livingstone also kept careful notes of his journeys and wrote a journal. At that time people did not know very much about the central areas of Africa. Livingstone hoped that his travels would help open up the country, so that other types of trade could replace the slave trade. He also hoped by opening up the country, that Christianity would be able to spread. He believed that the teachings of Christ would help to bring peace and would end the slave trade.

"Chuma, these books and letters are very important to me," Livingstone said to his companion as he sat outside his house in Ujiji. "If anything happens to me, try to get them to my friends in Zanzibar. They will be able to use this information to help end the slave trade."

As Livingstone travelled, he continued to talk about the slave trade with the chiefs and rulers that he met.

"We all have one Father. We are all children of the Mighty God. Therefore we should not sell each other. And look at the results… In order to have slaves to trade, there is constant fighting. No one is safe and everyone lives in fear. Unite with each other as one family against the slave traders. This trade in people is destroying the country and leaving it as a wilderness."

Not all the communities that Livingstone visited accepted the slave trade. Whenever he met a leader who rejected slavery totally or who helped to free enslaved people, he made a note of what he saw.

In August 1866, Livingstone wrote to his son.

> Dear Thomas,
> I have lost a lot of weight. We have only been able to shoot turtle-doves and guinea-fowls to eat.
>
> The last stage of our journey brought us to a fine country, with plenty of crops and healthy cattle. The principal chief of this area is called Mataka. His town contains a thousand houses. Many of these houses are square, just like the Arabs build their houses.
>
> When we arrived, Mataka was giving orders to send back people and cattle that they had stolen in a raid. This raid had been carried out without Mataka's knowledge and he demanded that they be allowed to return home. I saw fifty-four women and children, about a dozen young men and boys and about twenty-five or thirty head of cattle..."

Many of the Arab slave traders, did not steal or raid for slaves. Instead they lived in trading towns and villages, becoming friends with the local people. They then offered goods such as cloth, beads and brass rings in return for people. However, there were also many traders who were prepared to kill and to raid in order to enslave men, women and children. In April 1871, Livingstone was to see for himself one of these raids. His reports of this event were to have important consequences.

Livingstone's expedition had come to a halt. He had spent months getting to the Lualaba River and now he was stuck. The local people, the Manyuema, would not sell him canoes to cross the river. Some of his own porters were unhappy about crossing the river and encouraged the traders in the town not to help the British explorer.

Livingstone was frustrated. Day after day, he waited hoping that he might find a way to cross the river. Whilst he waited, he spent the time learning about the local people. Often he would go into the market, and spend the morning watching the traders selling their fish, cassava and clay pots.

One day Livingstone counted 700 people walking past his door on the way to market. Many of these people were woman. There was a local custom that protected the woman traders. Even when communities were fighting each other, it was forbidden to attack a woman on her way to market.

Then one morning, as Livingstone entered the market, he noticed something unusual. Three slave traders had their guns with them. Guns were not allowed in the market.

Suddenly, Livingstone heard a shot. The women in the market were terrified, dropped their baskets and ran towards the river in order to escape in their canoes. However, down by the river was another group of men who had begun to fire at the fleeing crowd. Even as people tried to swim across the river, they were shot by the traders. By the time the shooting had come to an end at least 330 people had been killed.

Livingstone tried to protect as many people as he could. Yet the fighting continued across the river with the burning of villages and the taking of captives. Furiously, Livingstone wrote down what he saw and scribbled letters describing the massacre.

After the fighting had stopped, Livingstone no longer wanted to ask for help from these Arab merchants. He was disgusted with what they had done. In the end, the explorer had to admit defeat and to abandon his plans to explore the region beyond the River Lualaba. He did not have enough supplies and without help from the merchants, he was forced to return to his base in Ujiji.

However, his letters and reports describing the massacre of the Manyuema people were published in Britain. As a result, the British Government set up a committee to investigate ways of stopping the slave trade within Africa. A decision was made to send Sir Bartle Frere to Zanzibar to start negotiations with the Sultan of Zanzibar to close the slave market.

Livingstone pulled himself onto his donkey. However, within a few steps the exhausted man lost his balance and slid on onto the ground. Chuma dropped his gun and ran to stop the other people in the expedition from going on further.

"Chuma, I am bleeding too much. There is no more strength left in my legs." Chuma kneeled down at the side of the frail, old man. The last few weeks had been a strain for everyone in the expedition as they had marched through endless swamps. Heavy rainfall had drenched the travellers, their equipment and supplies. Livingstone was also suffering from severe dysentery, and yet he wanted to continue his journey.

"You will have to carry me," he instructed his porters.

However, within a few days, Dr. Livingstone was dead. This came as no surprise to Chuma and the other leaders of the expedition. They were prepared and knew what had to be done.

"We must take his body to the coast. The people in his country will need to know that he is dead. But we will bury his heart here, where he has lived and died," Susi, one of the expedition party, explained to the others.

"What about his letters? We must also take his letters with us," Chuma added, remembering the Doctor's wishes. Together the leaders of the group put his last letters and notes into a tin box, ready to take to the coast.

The journey back to the coast would take almost 10 months. On the way the men and women who carried Livingstone's body, met a group of

English men who were travelling to meet Livingstone. They encouraged Susi and Chuma to bury David Livingstone, but the two men refused.

"The Doctor's body must be returned to his country," Chuma insisted.

Susi spoke to one of the English officers, "You must go back to Ujiji. The Doctor has left a box there with his journals and notes. It must be collected as those journals contain important information."

The officers agreed and found them just as Susi had said. Livingstone's letters, notes and journals were used to write about his last journey and to describe the destruction caused by the slave trade.

When Livingstone's body was returned to Britain, he was given a state funeral. He is buried in Westminster Abbey. On his tombstone are written the words from one of his last letters about the slave trade:

"All I can add in my solitude is, may Heaven's rich blessing come down on everyone, American, English, or Turk, who will help to heal this open sore of the world."

At a Glance: David Livingstone

David Livingstone was a missionary and explorer in Africa. He hoped to bring Christianity and new sources of trade to African people. He believed that this would help wipe out the slave trade.

Born in Scotland in 1813, he worked as a child in a cotton mill, whilst studying at night. He became a Christian and decided to devote his life to relieving human suffering. As a result he trained to be a doctor and became a missionary.

Livingstone first worked as a missionary in South Africa and it was here that he began to see slavery for himself. One group of people in South Africa called Boers, considered black people to be inferior to white people. Many Boers used black people as slave labour.

Livingstone began to explore the central parts of Africa. Here he saw the awful effects of the slave trade. He began to write about what he saw to inform the general public and the British government.

On his visits back home, Livingstone wrote books about his travels and also spoke at meetings. He described the horrors of the slave trade and criticised the Portuguese for allowing the slave trade to continue in their territories.

After Livingstone's death, other people such as Sir John Kirk continued to fight for the end of the slave trade in East Africa.

Fact File: East Coast of Africa Slave Trade

1. For centuries, Arab settlements on the East Coast of Africa sold slaves to Islamic countries and to India. Merchants bought slaves and ivory from central Africa and exchanged them for guns, cloths and beads.

2. These traders usually bought captives from African tribes that had raided tribes in other areas. These raids also resulted in the death of thousands of people and in the destructions of homes and crops.

3. The slaves were marched to the coast. This walk could take months. 20% of the slaves died on the journey.

4. The centre for the slave trade was the island of Zanzibar. In the 1870's 20,000 enslaved people were being sold there each year.

5. In the year of Livingstone's death, 1873, the British Government negotiated with the Sultan of Zanzibar to end the trade of slaves. In 1873 the slave market in Zanzibar closed. In 1876 the Sultan promised to end slave export from Zanzibar. However, illegal trading continued.

Faith in Action

The people in this book worked towards a goal – the end of slavery. They had a dream of how society could change. Wilberforce saw his dream come true. Livingstone did not see the results of his campaign against slavery. However, he drew comfort from this verse in the Bible: 'Commit thy way unto the Lord; trust also in him; and he shall bring it to pass.' Psalm 37:5 KJV. Livingstone believed that his work and its outcome was in God's hands. God was in ultimate control.

We can commit our lives, dreams and struggles to God. Sometimes we do not see the results of our efforts. That does not mean we have failed. It only means that as a human being we are unable to see or understand everything that happens.

Talk About It

Think about these words in the New Testament: 'Let us not become weary in well doing, for at the proper time we will reap a harvest if we do not give up.' Galatians 6:9 Ask God to help you not to give up doing good when things get difficult. Can you think of ways to encourage yourself or other people to keep going and not to give in?

Make Your Voice Heard

Poverty remains one of the root causes of slavery. Poverty is when people do not have enough to eat, when children are unable to go to school, when people do not have homes, and when communities are unable to combat disease. The causes of poverty are complex: Unfair trade; HIV and AIDS; International Debt; War; Corrupt Government. Go to the web site page at the end of the book to see how you can make your voice heard by fighting poverty and slavery today.

Baroness Cox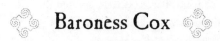

 HEADING TOWARDS A DUSTY RUNWAY, THE CESSNA
airplane began to lower its wheels. Although it was still morning,
the hot air rising from the ground caused the plane to bump
uncomfortably as it descended. Baroness Cox looked down at
the dry, flat land below. A few thorn trees provided some shade from the
African sun. She could see a small group of people watching patiently as
the plane came in to land.

"Everything ready?" Baroness Cox asked the journalist sitting
opposite, as she unbuckled her seat belt. He nodded and picked up his
camera. Stepping out of the plane, Baroness Cox felt the hot wind on her
face. Once again, she had arrived in Sudan.

Baroness Cox had been making regular trips to this southern part of
Sudan for a number of years. The isolated communities she came to visit
were suffering from the effects of a civil war that seemed to continue
without an end in sight. This war had resulted in the death of two million
people. Many more millions had left their homes in search of safety.

This time she was visiting an area that was only twenty miles from
where the Government of Sudan was fighting the Sudan People's

Liberation Army. The fighting in the area had caused many of the people who lived there to flee. Those who remained slept out under the trees at night, fearful that at any time they might be attacked again.

Reaching out her hand, Baroness Cox greeted the tall teenager. With a shy smile, the thirteen year old introduced herself.

"My name is Rebecca Nyam Mathok and I am a Dinka."

The Dinka people come from the south of Sudan, where traditionally they lived by herding cattle and growing basic crops.

That morning Rebecca had come to meet this English woman with one purpose in mind. She wanted to tell her story. Even though it would be difficult, she wanted people to know what had happened to her. With the help of a translator Rebecca began to speak:

"I became a slave three years ago in 1996…"

Rebecca looked up. She could hear a noise getting louder. A cloud of dust rose from the horizon. Horses! But it was too late to run. She looked around for her sister and grabbed Nyanabyei by the hand. Huddling together they watched as the armed raiders spread throughout the village.

Suddenly Rebecca could see smoke coming from the grass roof of her home. She held her sister back. It would be too dangerous to try and rescue their belongings. One of her uncles had grabbed a spear, but it was no match for the guns that the raiders carried. Now he lay dead on the ground.

A man pulled Rebecca to her feet and pushed her roughly towards a group of other women and children. One by one their hands were tied. Then they were made to march behind the horses. Rebecca walked with her head bowed as she left her village. All that remained was ruined, burning homes. Rebecca had become a slave.

"Stop crying!" shouted a tall man dressed in a long, white robe. Rebecca tried to stop the tears, but still her body shook. "I told you to stop crying!" the man shouted again, but this time he had picked up a stick. With a thud he began to hit her. Rebecca fell to the floor. However hard she tried, the tears would not stop.

Rebecca was now living with Mahjoub Hassan and his family. Every day Mahjoub and his wife forced her to work long hours. Sometimes she looked after the animals or worked in the fields. The rest of the time she had to wash, cook and clean. Every night she finished exhausted. That day Rebecca was feeling unwell, but still Mahjoub demanded that she went to look after the cattle.

"She's a worthless Dinka!" his wife sighed.

Rebecca had been sent to sweep. Backwards and forwards went the grass brush until the dust, which had blown in during the night, was pushed into the corners of the yard. Two of Mahjoub's younger children were laughing as they chased each other around the lime tree.

"Come and play with us!" one of them called. But although Rebecca watched them, she did not want to play. Playing was something she did at home, in her village with her sisters and cousins. Now there seemed no point. How could she join in with their laughter when all she wanted to do was to go home?

Mahjoub and his family were Muslims. Soon after her arrival he explained to Rebecca, "If you live with us, you must also become a Muslim."

At first Rebecca refused. She did not want to be a Muslim. She had been brought up as a Christian and did not want to change her religion. However, whenever she refused Mahjoub beat her.

All alone Rebecca was afraid; afraid of the beatings, afraid that she might even be killed. So Rebecca did what she was told and became a Muslim. However at night, as she tried to sleep out in the open, feelings of regret and sadness filled her mind. Watching the moon glide across the sky, she longed to be back home. She longed for her freedom again.

The years passed slowly for Rebecca. Then one day, Mahjoub's wife called her into the house. "Put this on!" she said handing her a brightly coloured piece of material called a tobe. As she wrapped the beautiful cloth around herself, she wondered whom she was meant to impress.

It was not long before she knew the answer. Under the lime tree, Mahjoub sat with a friend. They were laughing as they drank coffee from small porcelain cups. Rebecca was made to come forward and to greet the visitor. As she shook his hand, she recognised him as a neighbour.

Later that evening, the purpose of the visit was explained. "It will soon be time for you to be married," Mahjoub's wife informed her. Quickly, Rebecca turned away. Over the years she had learnt to hide the tears, to hold them back until she was alone.

However this time, Rebecca could not be silent. Calmly, she turned to face the older woman. "I do not want to marry him. He is so much older than me." Then she rushed out of the door.

Not long afterwards another visitor came and knocked at the blue metal gate. This time, Mahjoub did not welcome the visitor. Quickly the stranger was brought into the house and the door was pushed shut.

"You have a girl staying with you. Her name is Rebecca Nyam Mathok," the merchant paused. "She is a Dinka and her family wants her back. You have no right to keep her here."

"But I have cared for her for three years. I have fed her, clothed her. She is part of our family now. How can I let her go?" Mahjoub asked.

The merchant was ready with an answer.

"Her family will compensate you. They have the money to buy her back. I have to find her other sister. Then I will return with the money."

The stranger paused to look through the gate before he left the compound. The street was empty and so he slipped quickly away and headed towards the market.

Rebecca ran after him. "Take care!" the man warned her in a whispered voice. "Sometimes owners are afraid to release their slaves and will try and harm them. I am going to find your sister and then God willing, I will return to collect you all."

Rebecca took the visitor's advice. She was careful what she ate and drank in case it was poisoned. She worked hard so that Mahjoub did not become angry. And every day she watched, longing for the trader to return.

Finally the day came when the merchant did return with the money for her ransom. However, Mahjoub was still unhappy about letting her go. "Perhaps she doesn't want to go," he tried to argue. "She is about to get married to a good man."

"Go and ask her then!" replied the stranger.

Mahjoub found Rebecca cooking dinner on an open fire. "The trader is here," he told her. Rebecca stopped stirring the pot and stood upright.

"I am ready to go!" she announced and began to walk away.

Suddenly Mahjoub flew into a rage and grabbed Rebecca firmly. "The Dinka should not try to get their children back. You are part of my family now!" He raised his hand and hit her hard. For a moment she stumbled backwards.

"I want to leave!" she exclaimed. "I do not belong to you. I want to return to my own home. I want to go back to my own family."

Gradually Mahjoub lowered his hand. Looking into her face, he saw that she was determined to leave. The money that the merchant had brought would certainly come in useful. Perhaps it was time to let her go, he thought to himself.

Whilst Rebecca described the journey back to her village, she slowly began to smile. "It is so wonderful to be back home. Now I am free and can go where I want. No one can force me to do what I do not want to do. Now I am free to be a Christian."

As Rebecca finished her story, other people stepped forward to talk to Baroness Cox and the journalists who had come with her. Their stories told of armed men attacking their villages. These bands of men came to kill, steal and burn homes and crops. The animals, which were essential for people's survival, were either looted or shot. Women and children were taken away as captives to unknown places.

Baroness Cox took careful notes of everything she heard. As she wrote in her notebook, she felt horror and dismay at the tragic stories. Yet she was also amazed at the strength and determination she saw in people's lives.

As well as gathering facts, Baroness Cox wanted to show practical support to people experiencing these hardships and suffering. She was visiting Sudan as the President of Christian Solidarity Worldwide (CSW), a human rights organisation and had brought medical supplies to distribute.

In the town of Turalei, a doctor pointed out the marks of bullets on the clinic's wall. The previous year, the Government army had attacked Turalei. With very little equipment or medicine it was impossible to treat the many people who came for help.

Turning to Baroness Cox, the doctor remembered the events of the previous year when so many people had been killed. "Christian Solidarity Worldwide will be remembered in our history. You came last year when we had nothing and you gave us what we needed to save many lives."

Once again, Baroness Cox handed over boxes of basic medicine. The supplies would never be enough, but they would show the people of Turalei that the outside world had not forgotten them.

The other task that Baroness Cox had come to do was to give money so that slaves like Rebecca could be brought back to their families. For many years there had been an agreement that enslaved Dinka children could be bought back from their abductors at the price of five cows. However, for many Dinka families, who had lost their cattle because of the war, this was a price beyond their reach. In some of these cases Christian Solidarity Worldwide stepped in to help.

As Baroness Cox handed over a case of money, she knew that paying a ransom was not the answer to slavery in Sudan. Yet having listened to people's requests for help, she could not walk away and do nothing for those women and children who had been abducted from their homes.

The next day the Commissioner of the area met with Baroness Cox to discuss the problem.

"We want this war to be stopped. We want peace not war," he told her. "Yesterday you helped to achieve the freedom of 325 slaves. They need their freedom but this is not the ultimate solution. Perhaps tomorrow the raiders will come again and therefore the solution must be peace. Please do everything you can to stop this war."

On the plane back to Britain, Baroness Cox typed up the many notes that she had made onto a computer. For many years now she had been travelling to countries experiencing war or facing problems that needed international support. Her task was often to bring the facts of what was going on to the attention of the international community in order to obtain help for the people who were suffering. For a moment she stopped her typing and thought back to the time when it had all began.

In 1983 Baroness Cox had been asked to be patron of the charity, Medical Aid for Poland Fund. At that time Poland was a Communist country and life was very difficult. Hospitals were in desperate need of medical supplies.

"I want to get involved in a practical way," she explained to the charity. "Let me travel with the lorries into Poland. Then I will see for myself what life is like there and will be better able to help." So that is what she did. Baroness Cox travelled with the lorries, helping to take medical equipment and supplies to hospitals.

Then one night as she was passing through a forest, the lorry suddenly came to an unexpected stop. The driver opened his door and without a word disappeared into the darkness.

Alone and far from anywhere, Baroness Cox began to feel afraid. Pushing those thoughts away she decided to use the time to pray.

"Dear God, in this silence help me to listen to your voice."

As she prayed three words came into her mind, "Share the darkness".

When Poland finally became a free and democratic country, the Parliament wanted to thank Medical Aid for Poland for all their help. Baroness Cox attended the meeting. "Thank you for sharing our darkness," the government official said as he shook her hand.

Baroness Cox thought back to that night in the Polish forest. She remembered the words that had come into her mind and she knew that God was guiding her. Sharing people's darkness was to become Baroness Cox's work. Promoting human rights and speaking out on behalf of those experiencing war and oppression was to become her mission.

Now as President of Christian Solidarity, Baroness Cox was determined to share the darkness of people caught up in the war in Sudan. She did this every way she could: by newspaper articles, television reports and also by speaking in the House of Lords, part of the British Parliament.

Three months after hearing Rebecca's story of slavery in Sudan, she urged the British Government to take more action against modern forms of slavery.

"Will this Government follow in the tradition of William Wilberforce and make increased efforts to try to achieve an end to the terrible practice of slavery?" she asked the House of Lords.

However, Baroness Cox's attempts to highlight the situation in Sudan did not always go down well. As the news reports were broadcast, some people were unhappy about what they heard. A major argument broke out over the issue of slavery in Sudan. There were so many questions to answer.

Could there really be slaves in Sudan - after all it was the twentieth century? Were the reports accurate? Was the Sudanese Government involved and supporting slavery? Was the buying back of slaves actually making the problem worse? What was the best way to tackle the problem?

The Sudanese Government was particularly angry with Baroness Cox. "Slavery was abolished in 1924," they said. "It no longer exists in Sudan."

However slowly, due to growing international pressure, the Sudanese Government was forced to take some positive action. They still rejected the suggestion that there were any slaves in the country. However, they could no longer deny the evidence that proved that people were being abducted from the south of Sudan and being taken against their will to work for people in other parts of the country.

So the Sudanese Government formed a special committee. The job of the committee was to return abducted women and children back to their families, to bring to trial anyone involved in this crime and to find out how to stop such abductions happening in the first place.

It was not an easy task to find these missing people. However, the Dinka elders made lists of the names of people who had been abducted. Now, with the reluctant help of the government authorities, people on that list began to be found and reunited with their families.

Two years later, Baroness Cox and Christian Solidarity Worldwide stopped giving money to buy back slaves. They had drawn attention to the issue and now at last something was being done.

Every year in Sudan, people look forward to the end of the dry season. They watch for the clouds in the sky. They wait for the damp air to bring the rain. Then when the rain falls heavily from the sky, soaking the earth, people rejoice. They sing and celebrate for now the crops will grow and there will be food for the cattle. With the same eagerness, the people of Sudan watched and waited for the end of war, which finally came in January 2005. For only with the coming of peace, can there be lasting freedom.

At A Glance: Baroness Cox

Caroline Cox was born in 1937 and started her career as a nurse. She became a member of the House of Lords in 1982.

The House of Lords is part of the British parliament and is responsible for approving new laws put forward by the government.

In the House of Lords, she is well known as someone who speaks out about people suffering in countries where they are denied their human rights or are victims of war and injustice.

Baroness Cox has worked to improve human rights in many countries including Poland, Russia, Burma and Sudan. She is President of Christian Solidarity Worldwide – U.K., a charity that works on behalf of Christians suffering because of their beliefs. CSW also promotes religious freedom for all.

In January 1995 she received the Annual Wilberforce Forum Award in Washington. This award is given to people who show the principles and commitment of William Wilberforce by their actions.

Fact File: Modern Slavery

1. Today the word 'slavery' is used to describe traditional slavery, the slave trade and modern forms of slavery. These include: Forced labour; Bonded labour; Trafficking in persons; Worst forms of child labour

2. Bonded labour: This happens when someone owes a debt. That person then has to work for the lender of the money until the debt is repaid. Often, the interest and fees due on this debt become so great that the person is unable to earn enough to pay it back. Sometimes the debt is then passed onto their children, who then also become enslaved and have to work to pay back the debt.

3. Trafficking in Persons: This term describes how people are sometimes taken to other countries and made to work against their will. They are sometimes kidnapped or sold to the people who organise this crime. However, often these victims are promised well-paid jobs in a different country. When they arrive they find that these jobs do not exist. They end

up being exploited and controlled by the people who transported them. Their passports can be taken away and they find themselves enslaved.

4. Worst forms of child labour: This term describes any work that is dangerous for a child, stops him or her attending school, or is illegal.

Faith In Action

An important verse for Baroness Cox is *'Speak up for those who cannot speak up for themselves. For the rights of all who are destitute. Speak up and judge fairly; Defend the rights of the poor and needy. Proverbs 31:8.* Baroness Cox puts this verse into practice by speaking out about human rights abuses. Are we willing to speak up for justice and the rights of the poor?

Talk About It

Governments are trying to stop slavery through laws and agreements for example: The Universal Declaration of Human Rights; The UN Convention on the Rights of the Child; African Charter on Human and People's Rights. But this is not enough if the root causes are not dealt with such as poverty, discrimination, inequality and corruption. People need to be educated too. With international and national laws against slavery, why do you think it still exists? What is your Government doing to stop slavery?

Make your Voice Heard

Visit Anti-Slavery International (www.antislavery.org). Make your voice heard. You can campaign against modern slavery and its causes. You can support efforts to combat human rights abuses and injustice. Pray for God's help!

Author's notes

The stories told in this book are based on real people and real events. A few minor characters did not exist but their actions are consistent with evidence of what people did at that time. In other parts of the book, I have used my imagination to describe details of what may have happened in order to create a framework for the story.

In some places I have tried to use the written and spoken words of the actual people. However to ensure that the dialogue is easily understood by modern readers, I have condensed or changed the original words whilst trying to remain faithful to the intended meaning of the words. I have also not used the dialects and vocabulary that people may have used at the time. In order to keep the flow of the narrative, some of the dialogue is fictional.

In order to write this book I have consulted a wide range of sources. It is not possible to list them here, but wherever possible I have consulted original works and first hand accounts of what happened.

I would like to thank Christian Solidarity Worldwide for permission to use their document, Christian Solidarity Worldwide Trip Report (Sudan 15 -21 February 1999). Baroness Cox's story is loosely based on this report.

The fact pages at the end of each chapter are designed for personal study and for group discussion. References are made to organisations. These references are not endorsements of the organisations by Christian Focus Publications. Neither is Christian Focus Publications responsible for the content of Internet sites connected to these organisations.

I would like to express further thanks to:

Wilberforce House Museum

Merseyside Maritime Museum

Library of the Religious Society of Friends

Angus Library, Regents Park College, Oxford

I would also like to thank my husband, Andrew, and my daughters, Louise and Susanna, who gave me endless support whilst writing this book.

Websites

Antislavery websites should be reviewed by parents or guardians prior to being accessed by a child. What is suitable information for one child may not be suitable for another. While there is useful information on these sites there can also be graphic true life stories regarding contemporary slavery. Parents should be aware of what information is available through these sites before their children are allowed free access to them. We recommend that all websites be visited with parental supervision or guidance. This book is specifically aimed at ages 9-12, but websites must be treated with appropriate care. As always Christian Focus Publications does not necessarily advocate all opinions expressed on these sites and neither is it responsible for what is published on them.

Anti Slavery: www.csw.org.uk

        www.antislavery.org

        www.amnesty.org

        www.releaseinternational.org

        sb.od.org

        www.nmm.ac.uk/freedom/viewTheme.cfm/theme/timeline

        www.spartacus.schoolnet.co.uk/slavery.htm

Anthony Benezet: www.brycchancarey.com/abolition/benezet.htm

        www.pbs.org/wgbh/aia/part3/3p248.html

Olaudah Equiano: www.atomicage.com/equiano/life.html

        www.brycchancarey.com/equiano

Granville Sharp: www.spartacus.schoolnet.co.uk/REsharp.htm

        www.brycchancarey.com/abolition/sharp.htm

        en.wikipedia.org/wiki/Granville_Sharp

William Wilberforce: www.spartacus.schoolnet.co.uk/REwilberforce.htm

        justus.anglican.org/resources/bio/214.html

        www.britannia.com/bios/wilberforce.html

        www.brycchancarey.com/abolition/wilberforce.htm

Elizabeth Heyrick:	www.spartacus.schoolnet.co.uk/REheyrick.htm
	www.suite101.com/article.cfm/3550/26248
	www.spartacus.schoolnet.co.uk/REheyrick.htm
	rmc.library.cornell.edu/abolitionism
	www.setallfree.net/elizabeth_heyrick.html
	en.wikipedia.org/wiki/Slavery_Abolition_Act
Sam Sharpe:	www.cpy.org.uk/samsharpe/history.shtml
Harriet Tubman:	www.incwell.com/Biographies/Tubman.html
	www.nationalgeographic.com/features/99/railroad
	www.civilwarhome.com/tubmanbio.htm
	www.pbs.org/wgbh/aia/part4/4p1535.html
Harriet Beecher Stowe:	digital.library.upenn.edu/women/stowe/StoweHB.html
	xroads.virginia.edu/~MA97/riedy/hbs.html
	www.americancivilwar.com/women/hbs.html
	www.harrietbeecherstowecenter.org
David Livingstone:	home.vicnet.net.au/~neils/africa/livingstone.htm
	www.wholesomewords.org
	www.bbc.co.uk/history/historic_figures
	www.britannia.com/bios/livingstone.html
Baroness Cox:	www.acinc.org.uk/baroness_cox_risks_her_life.htm
	www.christianitytoday.com/tc/8r1/8r1075.html

Picture it and Get Interactive

To see interactive maps showing trade routes round the world in the 1600's and 1700's go to: www.eduplace.com/kids/hmss05/applications/imaps/maps/g5s_u3/index.html

www.nmm.ac.uk/freedom

To see a picture of Anthony Benezet go to: www.pbs.org/wgbh/aia/part3/3h257.html

Find out about how fashion supported humanitarian causes during the fight to abolish slavery by going to: www.portcities.org.uk/london/server/show/conMediaFile.5583/Slave-Emancipation-Society-medallion.html

www.wedgwoodmuseum.com/slave.htm

To look at a picture of slaves cutting sugar cane go to: www.imagesonline.bl.uk and search under sugar cane.

To look at a picture of slaves being punished by working on a tread-wheel go to the same site and search under tread-wheel.

To see a picture of a female slave being auctioned go to: www.picturehistory.com and search under slave auction.

To see a picture of a slave in a muzzle and read Olaudah Equiano's words about this practice go to: www.pbs.org/wgbh/aia/part1/1h308.html

To see a picture of Granville Sharpe helping Jonathan Strong go to: www.nmm.ac.uk/tradeandempire, click on Search Station and go to Trade and Empire, Click on Abolition and then the Thumbnails.

On this site you will also find pictures of John Newton; William Wilberforce; Thomas Clarkson; William Pitt. You can also try your hand at the interactive Trade and Empire Quiz.

To see a map of the United States of America prior to the civil war go to: www. learner.org/biographyofamerica/prog10/maps

To view an interactive map/timeline of the free and slave states go to: www.learner.org/biographyofamerica/prog10/feature/index.html

To see pictures of slavery today go to:www.antislavery.org. Find out about Rita from India and João from São Paulo State, Brazil by going to the Education site and activities for the classroom.

VOICES AGAINST SLAVERY SOURCES

A brief sketch of the life and labours of Mrs. Elizabeth Heyrick, Crossley & Clarke, 1862.

ALIE, J.A., A New History of Sierra Leone, Macmillan, 1990.

ANTI-SLAVERY INTERNATIONAL:

"Forced Labour in the 21st Century"; "Is there slavery in Sudan?", 2001.

BENEZET, A., Some Historical Account of Guinea; Its Situation, Produce and the General Disposition of its Inhabitants, Kessinger Publishing.

BLAIKIE, W., The Personal Life of David Livingstone, 1910, (www.gutenberg.org).

BLOOM, H. (ed.), Harriet Beecher Stowe's Uncle Tom's Cabin, Chelsea House, 1996.

BOYD, A., Baroness Cox A Voice for the Voiceless, Lion Publishing, 1998.

BRADFORD, S., The Moses of Her People Harriet Tubman, Citadel Press, 2001.

BRENDLINGER, I., "Anthony Benezet: True Champion of the slave", Wesley Centre for Applied Theology, http://wesley.nnu.edu.

BROOKES, G.S., Friend Anthony Benezet, University of Pennsylvania Press, 1937.

CLARKSON, T., The History of the Rise, Progress and Accomplishment of the Abolition of the African Slave Trade by the British Parliament. (www.fullbooks.com)

CLIFFORD, J. (ed.), The English Baptists, who they are and what they have done, Malborough & Co, 1881.

CLINTON, C., Harriet Tubman The Road to Freedom, Black Bay Books, 2005.

COUPLAND, R., Livingstone's Last Journey, Collins, 1945.

DODDRIDGE, P, The Rise and Progress of Religion in the Soul. (www.ccel.org)

DUBOIS, The Philadelphia Negro, 1899. (www2.Pfeiffer.edu)

DUGARD, M., Into Africa, Bantam Press, 2004.

EDWARDS, P. (ed.), Equiano's Travels, Heinemann, 1996.

EQUIANO, O., The Life of Olaudah Equiano, or Gustavus Vassa, the African, Dover Publications, 1999.

EVERETT, S., History of Slavery, Bison Books, 1978.

HEYRICK, J.D., Harriet Beecher Stowe a life, OUP, 1994.

HINTON, J., Memoir of William Knibb, 1847.

HOCHSCHILD, A., Bury the Chains, Macmillan, 2005.

HOUSE OF COMMONS, "Report from the select committee on the extinction of slavery throughout the British Dominions, 1833.

HOLLETT, D., Passage from India to El Dorado, Associated University Press, 1999.

JEAL, T., Livingstone, Heinemann, 1973

LARSON, K.C., Bound for the Promised Land, Random House, 2004.

LEAN, G., God's Politician William Wilberforce's Struggle, Darton Longman & Todd, 1980.

LIVINGSTONE, D., The Last Journals of David Livingstone in Central Africa, Vol I & II, London, 1874.

LIVINGSTONE, D., A Popular Account of Dr. Livingstone's Expedition to the Zambesi and its Tributaries, (as published by www.gutenberg.org).

MALMGREEN, G., Religion in the lives of English Women, 1760 - 1930.

MIDGLEY, C., Women against slavery, Routledge, 1992.

NEWMAN, S., The African Slave Trade, Franklin Watts, 2000.*

NORTHCOTT, C., All God's Chillun, Edinburgh House Press, 1940.

OLDFIELD, J.R., Popular Politics and British Anti-Slavery, Frank Cass, 1995.

PAYNE, E.A., Freedom in Jamaica, 1933.

PETRY, A., Harriet Tubman Conductor on the Underground Railroad, Harper Trophy, 1996.*

POLLOCK, J., Wilberforce, Lion Publishing, 1977.

JANNEY, R.P., Harriet Tubman, Bethany House, 1999.

SCHREINER, S.A., The Passionate Beechers, John Wiley, 2003.

SEAVER, G., David Livingstone, his life and letters, Lutterworth, 1957.

SIMON, K., Slavery, Hodder and Stoughton, 1930.

SOCIETY OF FRIENDS "Quaker biographies Anthony Benezet", 1909.

STANLEY, B., The history of the Baptist Missionary Society 1792-1992, TT Clark, 1992.

STANLEY, H., How I found Livingstone in Central Africa, London, 1890.

STOWE, C., Life of Harriet Beecher Stowe, 1889, (www.gutenberg.org).

STOWE, H. B., A key to Uncle Tom's Cabin, Jewett, Proctor & Worthington, 1853.

STOWE, H. B., Uncle Tom's Cabin, Wordsworth, 1995.

TINDALL, P.E.N., History of Central Africa, Longman.

THOMAS, H., The Slave Trade: The History of the Atlantic Slave Trade 1440-1870, Macmillan Publishers, 1997.

WADE, R., Slavery in the Cities, The South 1820 - 1860, OUP, 1964.

WALVIN, J., England, Slaves and Freedom 1776 - 1838, Macmillan 1986.

WRIGHT, P., Knibb "the Notorious", Sidgwick & Jackson, 1973.

VAUX, R., Memoirs of the life of Anthony Benezet, 1817.

VERNEY, P., Slavery In Sudan, 1997.

Research at: The Wilberforce House Museum, Hull,

Merseyside Maritime Museum

Freetown, Sierra Leone

*Denotes books written specifically for children

Author Information

Catherine House has written many books, most of which have been published for the African market. One of her titles was translated into seven Zambian languages. She lived in Africa for many years although she is now living in Oxfordshire, England.

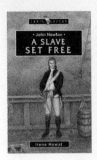  

John Newton: A Slave Set Free
ISBN 1 85792 8342

John Newton was one of the worst abusers of the African slaves as he travelled the oceans to make money from their misery, but this one time slave ship captain went on to speak out against slavery. Find out how God can carry out a transforming work in even the unlikeliest of hearts, when we least expect it.

William Wilberforce: The Freedom Fighter
ISBN 1 85792 3715

One man stood out from the many who sought to bring freedom and relief from the terrors of the slave trade: though it took him forty-five years to see it outlawed. William Wilberforce saw the abolition of all slavery in British territories become a reality just four days before his death on 29 July 1833. His story deserves to be told!

Mary Slessor: Servant to the Slave
ISBN 1 85792 3480

Mary Slessor had a shocking temper and a hard life. Living in a cramped tenement building with an alcoholic father was normal for her. But God had other plans for this young girl. Educating herself through reading and evening classes Mary eventually joined the mission and was sent to the Calibar region of Africa in present day Nigeria. God used Mary by sending her to those headhunting tribes that all the other missionaries were too afraid to visit. Courageous, plucky and impulsive it was said that even chiefs trembled when Mary's eyes flashed.

Christian Focus Publications publishes books for adults and children under its three main imprints: Christian Focus, Mentor and Christian Heritage. Our books reflect that God's word is reliable and Jesus is the way to know him, and live for ever with him. Our children's publication list includes a Sunday school curriculum that covers pre-school to early teens; puzzle and activity books. We also publish personal and family devotional titles, biographies and inspirational stories that children will love. If you are looking for quality Bible teaching for children then we have an excellent range of Bible story and age specific theological books. From pre-school to teenage fiction, we have it covered! Find us at our webpage: www.christianfocus.com